T0248263

FIRST
LIGHT

FIRST LIGHT

A JOURNEY
OUT OF
DARKNESS

LUCAS MATTHIESSEN

Arcade Publishing · New York

Arcade Publishing books may be purchased in bulk at special discounts for sales promotion, corporate gifts, fund-raising, or educational purposes. Special editions can also be created to specifications. For details, contact the Special Sales Department, Arcade Publishing, 307 West 36th Street, 11th Floor, New York, NY 10018 or arcade@skyhorsepublishing.com.

Arcade Publishing® is a registered trademark of Skyhorse Publishing, Inc.®, a Delaware corporation.

Visit our website at www.arcadepub.com.

10 9 8 7 6 5 4 3 2 1

Library of Congress Cataloging-in-Publication Data is available on file.

Jacket design by Brian Peterson

Print ISBN: 978-1-956763-31-7
Ebook ISBN: 978-1-956763-32-4

Printed in the United States of America

For Claire, with all my love

Acknowledgments

I AM FOREVER INDEBTED TO MARIA MATTHIESSEN AND JED HORNE for the guidance and encouragement which saw the manuscript past a first draft. Special thanks to Liz Van Hoose and Clementina Esposito for their keen insights and editorial acumen. My deepest gratitude to Jonathan Becker for his gift of the jacket photo and a lifetime of friendship. Lastly, this book could not have been written without the patience and unflagging support of Claire de Brunner, my dear wife and copy editor extraordinaire.

One

THE LIGHT PIERCED MY SKULL IN A SILENT EXPLOSION. I LET OUT a muffled groan but could do nothing to escape the pain. Fully dilated, my eye offered no defense, and his large hand pinned me to the headrest. My breathing quickened and tears began to stream down my cheek, but I made no further sound as the light continued to pummel my brain.

"Look up," the doctor said. He hadn't finished the second word before I complied, grateful for the brief respite. The light followed my eye, but the indirect angle was more forgiving than the frontal assault.

"Down," the doctor said. I had sensed the slightest movement of the light before he spoke, a slow scan with intermittent pauses, and the light brought closer as if to get a better look, to establish certainty before moving on. After looking down I again felt the probing, the light moving in and out, illuminating recesses never before explored.

My breathing slowed with the lessening of direct light into my pupil, and I released my grip on the armrests. I felt his breath on me, warm and rhythmical. "There is clear evidence of permeation, and I assume this will be consistent with the electroretinogram."

He shifted his position on the stool, rolling himself to the side before adding, "Look left."

I had closed my eyes while he moved, the darkness as soothing as a clove on an exposed dental nerve. The scope continued on its slow journey, the doctor occasionally pulling my lids farther apart to counteract my involuntary resistance. "It appears there is more pigment in the lower quadrants, and . . . how old is he again?"

"Twenty, Doctor," a voice said, following a rustle of paper.

"Yes," the doctor replied, "that would seem to be consistent. Look right," he added.

As before, I obeyed at once, my anxiety beginning to rise. His tone was that of one whose hypothesis has been confirmed, whose analysis has removed any residual doubt. His assessment of this last section, if not exactly cursory, was briefer, as if the relevant facts had already been established.

"Look straight ahead, please," he said quietly, and the same irrepressible pain erupted in my left eye. The light remained fixed as I stared into it, sweat beginning to form on my forehead as the seconds mounted. "Keep your eye open and looking straight ahead," he commanded after I had averted my gaze by no more than one or two millimeters. At last he relented, and the same sequence was repeated. "I want all of you to look at this," the doctor said as he turned off the scope and stood up. "The left eye shows a greater concentration of pigment in all four quadrants, and I'm guessing this was reflected in the visual field?"

"Yes, Doctor," another voice confirmed. "The peripheral range is considerably reduced in comparison to the right eye."

I sat back in my chair, my eyes closed as I wiped the tears from my cheeks. Someone turned on the overhead fluorescents, and the small room was suddenly filled with too much light as well as too many people. While Dr. Berson conferred with his staff, comparing the findings of the many tests I had undergone with his own examination, I glanced at my mother and sister, who sat upright and motionless in a corner. Both attempted weak smiles, but none of us spoke.

He had entered at the end of a long and arduous day like a victorious general, trailed by a retinue of worshipful subordinates and students. Dr. Eliot Berson carried himself in every way like the "great man," and it was obvious that he expected to be treated as such. He exuded an arrogant self-assurance, like one who was certain he would find the cure for this particular problem of human genetics and be justly awarded a Nobel Prize.

Ending the brief conference with his staff, he returned to my chair. "Well, I can confirm the diagnosis of retinitis pigmentosa," he said. "Your doctor in New York was wise to refer you to me. There is significant deterioration in retinal functioning, as has been verified by the tests we have run today, and I'm not surprised to hear that you are symptomatic."

"You mean the night blindness, Doctor?" I asked.

I had already developed a deep dislike for the man. Barely acknowledging our presence when he arrived, he asked his staff about the test results, whether certain information had been compiled, and whether I might be a suitable subject for study. The diagnosis had been delivered with the same bluntness, with no attempt at empathy or understanding. I steeled myself against him in response, adopting my best tough-guy "you're not going to hurt me" stance. I was determined not to be cowed, not to give in to him in any way.

"Yes," he replied. "That and a fairly significant shrinking of your peripheral field. You reported occasionally having difficulty locating objects, and I'm not surprised to hear that. Now, if you don't mind, I'd like my staff to examine your eyes. It's part of their training, you understand, and it would be very helpful to us."

"Of course," I replied with as much authority as I could muster, and the lights were dimmed again. They followed one after another, Dr. Berson enjoining each to pay attention to the patterns of permeation in both eyes, especially the accelerated deterioration of the left. I was like a butterfly on display, held in place by the examining light, without hope of escape or rescue. There were six of them in all, and the group kept up a running dialogue about my eyes as if they were disembodied, unattached.

When Dr. Berson was satisfied that everyone appreciated the intricacies of what they had just seen, he again sat on the stool next to me. Facing my mother and sister, he began to speak. "As I said, I can confirm the diagnosis of RP, and I don't believe any of my staff would disagree with that assessment." He paused just long enough to ensure that no one intended to contradict him before continuing. "I'm almost certain that yours is the X-linked variety, meaning that it is transmitted on the X chromosome from mother to son, much like sickle cell anemia." Without bothering to look toward his staff, he asked, "He has two male cousins with a similar syndrome, right? The mother's sister's sons?"

"Yes, Doctor," someone responded. "They're due to be tested next month."

"Good," Dr. Berson replied. "Like I said. X-linked, almost without a doubt." Turning to my mother, he said, "I'd like you to send me a family tree, to go back as far as you can to see if there is any evidence of blindness in your genealogy. This is very important."

"All right," she replied, barely above a whisper.

He shifted his gaze toward my sister. "I'm fairly sure you are a carrier. I mean, if my hypothesis is correct, your sons would have a fifty-fifty chance of having the condition. Do you have any children?"

"No," Carey replied.

"Are you married? Do you plan to have kids?"

"No, not yet," she said.

"Well, if you do, I'd like to examine them. Boy or girl, but particularly a boy. We're beginning to look at early intervention therapies, and it is important to get baseline data as soon as possible."

After a moment, as if he had almost forgotten to mention it, he added, "By the way, should you ever have an abortion, I'd like the material. It would be invaluable for study."

"All right," my sister murmured. I was outraged but said nothing. We were defenseless against him, overwhelmed by the brutality of his scientific certainty.

Dr. Berson kept silent as my mother and sister began to sob, head down and hands clasped between his legs. He looked pained, like he was waiting for one of us to ask for the solace he knew he couldn't provide. I would later understand that, as a research scientist, he may have lacked an intuitive appreciation of "bedside manner" and when to apply it. But in that moment he struck me as unfeeling, cold, uninterested in anything unrelated to finding a cure and securing his glory.

At last my mother rescued everyone from the terrible quiet, a silence broken only by the hum of the fluorescent lights. "What does all this really mean, Doctor? What's happening to Luke?"

"Are you referring to the specifics of the syndrome?" Dr. Berson asked, noticeably relieved to be back on empirical ground. He was at once energized and enthusiastic, eager for an answer in the affirmative.

"Yes, I suppose so," my mother replied, obviously confused.

"There are different genetic types of retinitis pigmentosa," he began, "as you may know. Again, I have every reason to believe that yours is the X-linked variety, this to be confirmed once I've examined the two cousins." Warming to his topic, he continued, "To put it most simply, RP, as its name would suggest, is characterized by the permeation of the retina with pigment. We believe this to be the result of reduced blood flow to that part of the eye, a process which eventually kills the rod and cone cells, those responsible for the transmission of light and color images to the brain."

Pausing, he asked, "Are you with me so far?" Tentative nods accompanied our mumbled confirmation. "The primary symptomology is the night blindness Luke referred to earlier and a reduction of the peripheral field. The vision loss begins at the outer range and moves toward the center, a phenomenon some-times referred to as 'tunnel vision.' If you hold up a cardboard tube to your eye, you'll get a good idea of how it looks to the patient."

Again assuming my hard-boiled facade, I asked, "And how is all this going to affect me, Doctor? I mean, specifically, exactly."

Dr. Berson paused before responding. "I understand that you're in college now. What are you studying? What career would you like to pursue?"

"I'm an English major," I replied. "I hope to become a writer."

"I see," he said. He hesitated, his eyes on mine. "I'm not sure that would be the best choice for you." Although his manner was still businesslike, his tone flat, I detected for the first time an undercurrent of regret, a softening of the scientific armor.

In the ensuing silence I recalled riding in my father's Land Rover five years earlier, returning to his house in Sagaponack after clamming near Sag Harbor. He was focused on the road, his mouth set, firm but relaxed. His silence and unwavering gaze signaled that he was thinking, weighing his next words, or that his mind was already back on his work. I couldn't see his eyes behind his sunglasses. Clad in an ancient tennis shirt, a damp blue bathing suit, and the Greek sailor's cap he always wore in 1968 (his John Lennon hat, as I called it), his six-foot-two frame appeared even larger inside the truck.

"I have a vision of a grand threesome of Matthiessen writers," he said as we crossed the Montauk Highway. More than his own father, he admired the legacy of F. O. Matthiessen, my grandfa-ther's cousin. The author of *The American Renaissance*, he had been one of the most distinguished scholars of his day.

My father didn't turn to look at me. His words seemed to give substance to the air, and neither of us spoke as the Land Rover gained speed. As a young man I was awed by him. What he had already accomplished was impressive enough, and now his burgeoning success was propelling him to an even more exalted plane. He aspired to write as well or better than Faulkner, and to take his place as a great American novelist would remain his highest ambition. I was beginning to fear that I had no hope of ever measuring up, that I was destined to be a disappointment. I certainly hadn't given any thought to becoming a writer, far less a peer of Faulkner, whom I hadn't read. Nor had I so much as opened any of the volumes bearing the name of Matthiessen. His directness was as surprising as his faith in my ability to become the third pillar of his triumvirate. I had always wanted to please him, and now he had voiced his belief that I was worthy and ready to fulfill my destiny. Like an underground river, those words would continue to course through my life, at times rising close enough to irrigate the surface before receding again into the depths.

"What's your prognosis, Doctor?" The question had come out not so much as a challenge, delivered with my chin thrust forward, but evenly, as if I were another physician seeking his opinion. Although I could hear my heart beating as he looked at me, I felt something give way, a relinquishing of my antipathy toward him.

"I would estimate, based on the tests we have run and the typical course of the condition, that you will have some sort of operative vision until the age of thirty-five or so," he said. "This is a preliminary estimate, of course, but I'm reasonably certain given your profile."

I felt like I had been gut shot, and fought back rising panic. I hadn't thought this possible, had never imagined I would go blind. I had lost some vision, I knew, and might well lose more, but to go blind, to lose "operative vision," had been unthinkable. In that moment I couldn't look at anything but his eyes, and I fought back a sudden surge of nausea. *This can't be true*, I told myself. *This can't be true*. I held his eyes, saying nothing, trying to compose myself. It was as if I were afraid to look away, that only by holding his gaze might he correct himself and declare that there was a good chance of maintaining some working vision for the rest of my life. My mother began to cry again, and I looked over to see my sister take her hand. No one spoke, and I was sure that every eye in the room was on me.

"Can you give me some idea of the progression, Doctor, and what you mean by 'operative vision?'" Without knowing why, I had let go of all resentment, and my outraged indignation had vanished. Though not conscious of it in that instant, I was beginning to appreciate that, his manner notwithstanding, Dr. Berson was probably the only person who could help me.

"You will experience an ongoing reduction of your visual field. Do you drive?" When I affirmed this with a nod, he continued, "Well, you should stop right now. It's not safe. Any remaining night vision will also diminish over time. Eventually, of course, your eyes will, for all practical purposes, cease to function. You may still see some light and shade, maybe even maintain a severely narrowed peripheral field, but I don't think this likely. That's why I'm encouraging you to reconsider your choice of career. Your vision loss will be gradual, but you should plan accordingly."

"Thank you, Doctor," I said. "That's very helpful." Perhaps intuiting that I had dropped my defenses, he came closer, as if we were suddenly alone in the room.

"I know this must be hard to hear, Luke," he said, "but as your doctor I need to present you with the facts. It's your life to live, but you need to know what you'll be facing to make the best choices."

Referring to himself as my doctor won me over, removed all traces of residual anger. I might have reacted differently, been offended by his presumption of intimacy or importance, but I was drawn to him then, and I forgave him everything.

Leaving his office that night, my mother and sister were indignant. Berson was cold, rude, unfeeling, a monster. Imagine asking for the "material." Didn't he appreciate how vulnerable we were, how important it was to mitigate the blow of the diagnosis? They were right, of course, and Dr. Berson later received a letter, signed by hundreds of his patients, expressing their collective distress over his lack of empathy. I never saw the letter, but wouldn't have signed it if given the choice. Yes, he was arrogant and grandiose, brusque, and even brutal. But what was more important, at least to me, was his dedication. Even if only for the sake of guaranteeing his own celebrity, he was committed to finding a cure. Above all else he was a scientist, not a general practitioner, and I took comfort in that. Before leaving the hospital I had put my trust in him.

We drove back to my uncle's house after dark, the last remnants of a November snow lining the road, and my family did what they could to console me. Everyone declared their love, coupling their embraces with heartfelt promises of support, and we agreed that I should return every year in case Dr. Berson developed an experimental treatment. As inhuman as he was in everyone else's eyes, there wasn't any other practical choice, not in those days.

My mother was nearly overcome with guilt. She had passed on the gene, as had my Aunt Sarita to her two sons, and couldn't let go of the conviction that she had inadvertently ruined my life. I reminded her that no one had known about this terrible problem lurking in our DNA, and she was not to blame for its emergence in my generation. While she could appreciate this logic, it did little to ameliorate her suffering. I reassured her that I would be fine, that Dr. Berson might find a cure, that I still had fifteen years of vision and that somehow it would all work out.

I was enormously relieved when everyone went to bed, and I was at last left to myself. So much attention had been focused on me throughout the day, and it felt good to be out of the spotlight. Before settling into an armchair next to the fireplace, I fetched a half-gallon bottle of vodka from my uncle's bar. A single lamp burned at the far end of the living room, and the house was cold.

There was no sound other than an occasional passing car and the ticking of a grandfather clock.

At first I was more numbed than dispirited. Sipping the vodka, which I drank neat, I wondered what I could look forward to as a blind man. I thought of Karen, my first great love, how beautiful she was, how an alluring tint of green could sometimes be seen when the sun shone through her blonde hair. Would she ever want to be with me if I needed a white cane? Would anyone? I recalled driving my friend Jonathan's father's old Triumph along the back roads between Amagansett and Southampton, its engine roaring in the predawn quiet. I loved to drive, play tennis, look at women, read a book.

But what would happen when I couldn't read? How would I earn a living? Jonathan was spending his nights at Elaine's, taking pictures of the proprietor with the countless celebrities who came to the restaurant like pilgrims to Mecca. Honing his craft, he would go on to become a photographer for *Vanity Fair* and publish several books. Would I be reduced to weaving samplers at the Industrial Home for the Blind? Horrified by that prospect, I quickly refilled my glass.

I recalled my photographs of Karen, the series I did on Little Italy, the landscapes, the portraits of the poets, musicians, and artists who frequented my stepfather's studio. All of it.

Everything I loved about my life involved sight. I remembered the harsh beauty of the desert mountains in Afghanistan, a faint glimpse of Everest at dawn, my old friend Jackie's smile, and the late afternoon light on the ocean. How would I experience beauty? What would it be like when I could no longer see the sky, Jonathan's extraordinary photographs of Coney Island in winter, or the paintings of almost all the adults I had grown up with?

Nothing I was passionate about, with the exception of music, seemed destined to be a part of my future. Looking ahead, I could see nothing but blankness, a half-life as half a man, an existence devoid of any real pleasure or fulfillment. In that moment I nearly lost all hope, fearing that my life would effectively be over in just a few years. What the hell would I do with myself? What would be the point?

The tears came at last, silent and slow, unseen by anyone. I was so alone, certain of nothing. I felt like the wind had been knocked out of me, like I was struggling to breathe. Could anyone point the way and provide the reassurance I had given my mother, that everything would work out in the end?

There had to be a path to some sort of meaningful life. As the clock chimed the eleventh hour I had no idea what that might look like, aware only of the joys that would be closed off, one after another, as the curtain came down. Despite my inability to picture an existence without sight, I recalled Dr. Berson's suggestion that choices were open to me. The alternative, a life devoid of possibility, was too terrible to imagine, but was it safe to believe him?

Reflecting on the day, I thought again of that morning in Sagaponack. I had last written my father after returning from East Africa. He was conducting some of the research which would eventually appear in *The Tree Where Man Was Born*, and had invited my sister and me to join him for two weeks during spring break. The letter was an expression of wonder and gratitude for what he had shown us, but I hadn't thought it especially noteworthy. What would I write about? Africa was still fresh, but could I ever hope to rival his work?

I recalled staring up at a leopard in an acacia tree on the Serengeti, his magnificence framed by the sharp yellow light of sunset; the trumpeting of an elephant as she charged, ears flapping, after we had inadvertently separated her from her calf; hundreds of flamingos standing in the shallows of Lake Manyara, their reflections casting a rosy hue over its surface; the astounding beauty of a young Masai woman cradling her child as she stepped into our Land Rover; and climbing out of Olduvai Gorge to find a giraffe standing not more than twenty yards away, both of us momentarily frozen by our unexpected proximity.

At that moment, another part of the ride back to Sagaponack rose to the surface, a recollection which would remain in conscious memory. As I waited for my father to emerge from the post office, the huge head of a Great Dane appeared just beneath my window. Although he was almost tall enough to poke his nose inside, I hadn't seen him coming. By night's end, I had finished nearly half the bottle.

The next morning's hangover was a relief, a welcome distraction, but the brief flicker of hope had vanished. If anyone noticed how much I had drunk, they didn't mention it. We flew back to New York that afternoon with the knowledge that our lives had been fundamentally altered.

I returned to Columbia determined to further my goal of becoming a writer. Ignoring Dr. Berson's good counsel, I forged ahead as if his prognosis had never been delivered. Like a plow horse with blinders on, I plodded through the spring semester of my sophomore year, occasionally bumping into people. I worked hard but without much interest or enthusiasm, academic success doing little to dispel a sense of undirected somnambulance.

Two

AFTER TWO YEARS, I HAD ALL BUT COMPLETED THE COLLEGE'S required courses and began to focus on my major. In the reading room above the library's lintel, I settled each day into a heavily cushioned leather armchair like an astronaut in a one-man space capsule. Marlowe, Chaucer, Pope, Milton, and others opened new worlds as I took notes and underlined innumerable passages, learning to decipher language and metaphor, context and style. I was always happy to be transported for a few hours before returning to the twentieth-century realities of Morningside Heights and my worsening vision.

Lionel Trilling was the great don of Columbia's English department, and I decided to apply for admission to his course on the romantic poets. On the appointed day a department secretary directed a long line of hopefuls, including me, to fill out a four-by-six index card listing our qualifications for consideration.

When I finally sat across from him, Trilling glanced at my card and asked whether I was related to F. O. Matthiessen. He looked tired, with dark circles under slightly sunken eyes and dull gray hair. After confirming my kinship, I confessed to knowing almost nothing about my esteemed relative. Leaning back in his chair,

Trilling informed me that, among other things, F. O.'s suicide was precipitated by his disillusionment over the prospects for world socialism. He had traveled to Eastern Europe in the early fifties, one of the first civilians to be granted access after the war, and returned thoroughly disenchanted. When he was subsequently denounced as a possible communist in the *Boston Globe*, he checked into a local hotel and jumped, leaving his Skull and Bones key on the windowsill.

I was fascinated by these revelations, no less surprised by Trilling's passion in relating them. He and F. O. had been contemporaries, and Trilling's respect for his peer was unbounded. After reviewing my card he closed the interview by declaring, "This looks fine, and you're wearing a tweed jacket. I like that. You're in the class."

My stepfather, Michael Goldberg, hosted a small dinner party a few weeks later. One of the guests, Hal Fonderin, was the director of the Poindexter Gallery and had first met my mother's closest friend, the poet Frank O'Hara, when they were schoolmates at Harvard. Hal was red-faced and affable, and his stomach betrayed his predilection for good food and drink. His blue blazer, elegant loafers, and electric orange tie gave him the appearance of a guest at an uptown soirée, not someone with close connections to the avant-garde crowd. But he had always been at the parties in my childhood home on 11th Street, far better dressed than everyone else.

I asked Hal whether he had known F. O. Matthiessen, and he recounted a night when one of Frank's plays was staged in Cambridge. After polite applause, F. O. stood up, turned to face the audience, and gently admonished them for not recognizing a work of genius. Hal went on to say that F. O. was loved by his students, and for a moment I keenly missed a man I had never met.

Peter Glassman, who had studied under Trilling a generation earlier, stood at approximately six feet, but a full head of unruly brown hair added another two inches to his appearance. He wore wire-rim glasses and usually sported a tweed or corduroy jacket. Registering for his course on Victorian literature that spring, I was at once drawn to his intelligence and insights into some of the more prescient themes in Carlyle, Arnold, and Eliot. From the first, although he was never sullen or outwardly depressed, I suspected there was somewhere a tragedy in Peter's life, that he carried a heavier burden than most. Sensing an undefined but powerful affinity, I quickly assigned him the role of mentor.

Until that point I had been increasingly despondent at Columbia, my interest in literature notwithstanding. Thinking that a change of scene might improve my outlook, I had even contacted Swarthmore to discuss a possible transfer. But the relationship I forged with Peter cemented a decision to stay, and for the first time I looked forward to returning in the fall.

That summer Jonathan's mother, Patricia Birch, was commissioned to choreograph the dance scenes in *The Wild Party*, a campy Merchant/Ivory adaptation of Joseph March's poem, and invited us to come along as extras. The film was shot at the Mission Inn in Riverside, California, a sprawling remnant of the town's better days, before the hot springs dried up. The second floor housed an ornate chapel where Nixon was married, and the hotel still rented it out for weddings. We were put up at the local Howard Johnson's, where every night the band recalled their own former glory by playing the theme song from *Gilligan's Island*.

The movie is absolutely forgettable, but we had a great time making it. Like everyone else, it seemed, I drank too much, snorted too much cocaine, and otherwise indulged in all the decadence which 1970s Hollywood had to offer. Pat Birch was heroic in her efforts to teach me the "Herbert Hoover Drag," and I can be seen at the end of that number falling to the floor with Raquel Welch.

After the filming, Jonathan and I borrowed my Aunt Sarita's station wagon at three in the morning and drove from Los Angeles to Mexico, inhaling a lot of coke and listening to Beethoven's Ninth at full volume as we barreled down the Pacific Coast Highway. We wound up at a seaside town in Baja called San Felipe, by which time our respectable suburban car was covered with dust and looked as if it made regular runs transporting migrants across the border. The next day vultures began circling overhead after I had lain on the beach for too long.

Toward the end of the summer I drove to Sagaponack for lunch and a swim. My father continued to travel regularly after the death of his second wife, Deborah Love, so I didn't see him more than two or three times a year. He was now living with Maria Koenig, a former model with long dark hair and an upper-class British accent who had been raised in East Africa. Maria had arrived with her two young daughters, Sarah and Antonia, and being with her always promised good conversation and fun.

Paul and Myrna Davis, close friends of Maria's I hadn't met, had also been invited. Paul had recently completed the posters for Joseph Papp's Public Theatre productions, and was recognized as one of the country's premier illustrators. A big man, he was soft-spoken, his face round and gentle. Myrna was good-natured and outgoing, a pretty woman with a perpetual smile. Spirits were high and laughter plentiful. After lunch my father and I cleaned up, grabbed two towels, and started out for the beach.

More cars were on the road by then, a sure sign that Sagaponack's days as a farming community were coming to an end. He had traded his Greek sailor's hat for an unadorned baseball cap, and his dark shirt and bathing suit looked old and loose on him. Breaking with the traditional protocol of our walks, he began our talk by telling me that he'd been inducted into the American Academy of Arts and Letters. To be recognized by his peers would always mean more to him than critical acclaim or financial success, and the best had now anointed him as one of their own. He was proud, and I was happy for him. Turning the focus back on me, he was excited to hear about my enthusiasm for literature.

As we neared the beach he put his hand on my shoulder and asked why I continued to drive. I'd told him everything after my trip to Boston, including Dr. Berson's warning that it was no longer safe to get behind the wheel, and had expected this exchange. He raised the question gently, with an intuitive appreciation of how loaded it was. Already bargaining with my fate—and perhaps to defuse exactly this kind of pressure.

I had stopped driving at night. He was glad to hear it, but before he could say anything more I insisted that I could still drive during the day. Pausing, he said he didn't think this wise, but I promised not to do anything foolish.

Elizabeth "Bumpy" Rogers, a beauty in her mid-thirties with large, smiling eyes, greeted us when we emerged from the ocean and asked my father when he might be free to play tennis. Bumpy had been one of his girlfriends following Deborah's death, but he broke it off after only a few months. When he replied that he was going on a Zen retreat in the morning, she turned to me. We had played several times and agreed to meet the following afternoon.

The next day was unusually hot. After two sets we were both tired, and Bumpy invited me to her house for a drink. Soaked with sweat, I could think of nothing better, and she made me a stiff gin and tonic before disappearing into the bathroom. When the door opened she stood naked before me, toweling off after her shower. Taking a long pull at my drink, I pondered my next move. As much as her seduction excited me, I knew this invitation carried significant risk. That my father would find out was more than likely, since they shared many friends. The logical thing was to excuse myself at once, but I said nothing as I stared at her. When she crossed the room and we kissed, I had already decided to roll the dice.

* * *

"What's Lukey doing here?" A child's voice, a little boy's voice. The room was unfamiliar, full of sunlight filtered through thin white curtains. Someone moved in the bed, and I heard Bumpy say, "It's all right, honey. Everything is okay. Luke is okay too. He's just sleeping now."

"But why is Lukey here?" the child asked again, the words slightly slurred. It was my brother Alex, then eight or nine, and the full weight of his presence hit me at the same moment I realized I had a staggering hangover. Feigning sleep, I tried to sort things out. I remembered almost nothing of the night before, only that we had gone out to dinner. I had no memory of her children, and none of my brother, their friend. Had he been there the whole time? Now it was certain that my tryst would get back to my father, and I pulled the covers further over my head.

I felt an overwhelming urge to disappear, get away, somehow erase the last twenty-four hours. At the end of this summer of extremes, I had now taken things too far. How would I explain this? What could I possibly say that would leave me with a shred of dignity?

Bumpy and I kept company for the next two weeks. We went to parties and were seen on the beach, making no effort to be discreet. I didn't feel any joy at the prospect of my father's return, but neither did I do anything to minimize the extent of my transgression. Although it was fun, I knew even then that the whole thing was foolish, ultimately empty, and impotent. We became the subject of local gossip, adding further insult to my father, and still it went on. Was that the point, to hurt or humiliate him as much as possible? I didn't think so, but couldn't deny that our cavorting would get his attention.

He demanded to see me as soon as he got back. The confrontation took place in his driveway, before I got to the door. "What were you thinking?" he asked.

"I don't know that I was thinking anything, Dad."

"I wouldn't have minded so much, though it was stupid enough, if Alex hadn't been a witness to everything. How could you be so thoughtless?"

"I'm sorry, Dad. It all just kind of happened . . ."

"No. Take some responsibility, Luke. From what I hear, you two were all over Sag Harbor together. Look, I really don't care who you sleep with, even an old flame of mine, but not like that. Not involving Alex and in front of my friends."

"It's over now, Dad, and I'm sorry about Alex. You're right. It was stupid. It won't happen again."

"You're damned right it won't," he said.

But it did. Before school started I drove Bumpy back to Chicago, the car packed tight with children and luggage. She came to New York several times in the fall, and we perpetuated what began to feel like an overplayed song. Finally, with a thousand miles between us, we ran out of gas and agreed to move on.

Our brief affair was anything but casual or arbitrary. Bumpy was obsessed with my father for decades after they separated, long after our fling was over. She would later be diagnosed with bipolar disorder, and maybe in some distorted way hoped to get to him through me. For my part, she was an attractive woman, and I was excited by the risk, the almost manic frenzy of the sex, drinking, and taboo. It was thrilling, at least in the beginning, and I didn't yet appreciate the extent to which I was apparently a means to an end. Being with Bumpy was like going to buy drugs, with the anticipation of danger and the special pleasure of illicit euphoria.

But apart from the allure of doing something wrong, always hard to resist in those days, I knew I was "sticking it" to my father. Perhaps I believed on some level that being with Bumpy put us on an equal footing, that sleeping with her represented a different sort of conquest. Dr. Freud, who might have danced a jig at the vision of my succumbing to her charms, would surely have pointed to good old Oedipus, not for the first time in my life, but I don't think my attraction was fueled by any incestuous fantasies.

In hindsight, I've come to see our liaison as a rite of passage, another means by which, however awkwardly, I was struggling to come into my own.

* * *

Before the start of my senior year, the dean's office reminded me that I still needed to take two semesters of physical education. The dean assured me that no waiver was possible if I hoped to graduate, so I signed up for fencing. Peter invited me to join him in teaching an advanced seminar on modern English literature. We discussed our ideas over coffee, settling on three writers we agreed were crucial to its evolution—Thomas Hardy, George Gissing, and, the focus of Peter's doctoral thesis, Joseph Conrad. The course was to be an in-depth review of the complete works of all three, with me taking the lead on Hardy and the two of us splitting duties on Gissing.

Seven students enrolled in the course, the perfect number for an intimate forum. Inspired, I worked hard, and partnering with Peter was deeply satisfying. At the end of the semester he commended me on my efforts and asked whether I'd given any thought to becoming an academic. Thanking him, I hesitated before replying that I wasn't ready to make any sort of commitment.

Continuing to ignore Dr. Berson's advice, I had done nothing to prepare for the inexorable progression of retinitis pigmentosa, burying all nascent reflections on my future as quickly as possible. I didn't speak of my impending blindness if I could avoid it, grateful that others rarely broached the subject. Living as if I weren't facing this grim reality, I couldn't deny the more frequent and alarming reminders of my decreasing ability to see. In spite of these, almost in defiance of them, I continued to drive, drank more than ever during academic breaks, and made my first attempts at controlled drinking during the school week.

These occurred not at the West End or some other popular college hangout, but at an inconspicuous dive called the Blue Marlin, on Broadway just north of 110th Street. Its patrons were almost always alone, rarely engaged in conversation except to ask the bartender for another round, and otherwise made it clear that they were there to drink, not socialize. Since this was also my modus operandi, I was content to sit in silence, sipping whiskey unobserved as I stared out the window.

That spring Peter nominated me for the Kellett Prize, a private one-year scholarship to Oxford. While honored, I arrived at my interview before the college's deans with another bad hangover. Holding things together well enough until they asked why I wanted to go to England, I paused before replying, "Well, wouldn't you?" I just couldn't think of anything else to say.

The next day Peter told me that I had been guaranteed the scholarship until that show of indifference, and I apologized. I felt I had let him down, but the prospect of another year of school— and the likelihood of several more to follow—suddenly seemed unthinkable.

As we walked down the hill to Riverside Park several weeks later, Peter informed me that Tulane had offered him a higher salary and full tenure. Columbia was fast becoming a conservative school, a shift being realized through the admissions department and the attrition of left-leaning liberal arts professors, so it was obvious that his future didn't lie in Morningside Heights. He felt he had no choice but to accept, especially since the extra income would help cover the cost of caring for his disabled son. Peter was disappointed by the university's reluctance to make a long-term investment in him, and the impending loss of an important mentor and friend cemented my own inclination not to pursue a life in academe. But since I had enjoyed teaching and had some basis for thinking that I might be good at it, I would occasionally regret that decision over the next fifteen years.

My last semester passed in a fog of confusion, clouded by uncertainty as much as drink. I continued to do well academically, and even satisfied the physical education requirement. Because I couldn't see my opponent's foil, I was hopeless at fencing, but managed to knock down a few pins on the bowling alley. George Plimpton, an old family friend who was the editor of the *Paris Review* and a man particularly sensitive to athletic underachievement, called just before my 1976 graduation.

"Of course you'll come work for the magazine," he said. Since I had done nothing to launch a career on my own, I accepted his offer on the spot.

Three

MY ONLY TACTILE CONNECTION TO A TIME BEFORE MY FIRST memory of either parent is an old black-and-white photograph, slightly yellowed and curled at the edges, taken beside a beached boat on Fishers Island. In the foreground my father is seen from behind, bending to look at his son. Then three or four, I am dressed in jeans and a turtleneck shirt, and holding an oar in both hands. Staring up at him, I look puzzled, or perhaps I am just squinting into the sun.

My parents, Peter Matthiessen and Patsy Southgate, were two of the American literary aspirants living in France in the early fifties. After he graduated from Yale and she from Smith, they married and moved to Paris. He became one of the "tall young men," as Irwin Shaw described that wave of American expatriates in Gay Talese's 1961 *Esquire* article, "Looking for Hemingway," and founded the *Paris Review* with Harold "Doc" Humes. They soon handed off the editorial stewardship to George Plimpton, the tallest young man, with whom my father had gone to grammar school.

Along with most of their friends, including William Styron and Terry Southern, they lived on the Left Bank, entertained a lot, and were at the center of the bohemian scene. They were young, smart, good-looking, and out to have a great time while staking their claim on the post-war literary landscape. I was born in the spring of 1953, arriving almost simultaneously with the first edition of the magazine.

We returned to the United States aboard the *Andrea Doria* on the voyage before it sank, perhaps the first instance of what my father would later point to as my lifelong tendency to court disaster. The second would come two years later, when I crashed the family car into the Amagansett post office after my mother ran inside, leaving the engine running and me free to clamber out of my car seat. No one was hurt, but the image of a red-faced man yelling in the window while Scoter, our black Labrador, panted in the back seat is my earliest memory.

My parents divorced in 1956, two years after the birth of my sister Carey, but their lives apart were no less compelling. With different values and aesthetics, their separate circles would become known as the "uptown" and "downtown" literary scenes, the "mainstream" versus the "avant-garde." I spent my childhood shuttling between those two worlds, each strictly associated with only one parent.

After their breakup, my mother moved to Springs, just north of Amagansett. Since both Jackson Pollock and Willem de Kooning had taken up residence there, it was already known as the cradle of abstract expressionism. Rents and property were cheap, and over the years more and more artists were drawn to the area. With sandy soil and patches of scrub woodland, Springs is loosely bordered by Gardiner's Bay, Three Mile Harbor, Amagansett, and the East Hampton town dump. There was nothing fancy about it when she arrived, the houses generally small and unassuming, and many "Bonackers," or those whose families hailed from the Accabonac Creek region, called it home.

In 1959, to my grandmother Southgate's great distress, my mother married the painter Michael Goldberg and purchased a four-story building in the West Village of New York City. She often joked that she married Mike just to piss off her mother, but there was a lot to love. In many ways Mike was the antithesis of my father. He wasn't reserved or reticent on any point, loved to use profanity and did it better than anyone I've ever known, would never be commended on the delicacy of either his manners or wit, and often dressed like a mobster. A tough guy from the Bronx, he was a veteran of the Pacific War. He drank too much, drove too fast, loved jazz and a good pastrami sandwich, and had the most impressive belch I ever heard. One of the "second generation" abstract expressionists, a group which included his best friend, Norman Bluhm, he had a scratchy beard and a lot of chest hair and usually smelled of cigarettes and alcohol. Fleeting aromas of turpentine or oils can still transport me back to his studio on East 10th Street, where I sometimes drew under a large skylight as he moved about in his paint-spattered overalls.

My mother arrived in France hardly knowing how to boil an egg. But because her looks gained her entry into the kitchens of her favorite Parisian restaurants, she would later be renowned for her mastery of *la gastronomie* as much as her beauty. Carey and I didn't appreciate the refinements of dishes like bouillabaisse or Coquilles St. Jacques, but whenever Mike raised the specter of moo goo gai pan if we didn't eat our dinner, the threat delivered in his best basso profundo, our forks always scurried across our plates.

I loved Mike almost as soon as he came into our lives. To me it felt like this was not only disloyal, but that I had somehow abandoned my father. Add to this my mother's thinly veiled antagonism toward him, and the secret truth that I was closer to Mike produced powerful feelings of confusion and shame which can still whisper to me, especially in dreams.

To some extent I am doubtless guilty of the same nostalgic romanticism which colors several chronicles of New York bohemian life in the late fifties and early sixties, those which portray an atmosphere of perpetual artistic innovation by day and uninterrupted revelry by night. But it did seem that a cocktail party was almost always in full swing during the seven years we lived on 11th Street, endless evenings when it was hard to move through our crowded living room. Everyone laughed and talked loudly, and Thelonious Monk or John Coltrane blasted from the record player as Mike emitted little percussive yelps and stomped his foot to the music. Not unlike that on Rue de Perceval, our apartment was a hub for the downtown art and literary scene. Along with Frank O'Hara, many contemporary poets, painters, and composers, including John Ashbery, Larry Rivers, and Lukas Foss, were regular guests in our home. By contrast, the literary enclave taking shape in Sagaponack, where my father bought his own house in 1960, eventually touted James Jones, Truman Capote, James Salter, John Irving, William Gaddis, and Edgar Doctorow.

Frank was always the central figure at my mother's gatherings, for me and everyone else, the one to whom we were most drawn. He was the personification of the party's excitement, charged by the energy of the moment. "Hey there, my best boy," he said when I climbed on to his lap. Frank was already balding by his mid-thirties. I loved the warmth in his high-pitched voice, and especially his laugh.

One night I offered to get him a drink when he emptied his glass, and he schooled me on how he liked it. Weaving my way toward the bar, I was greeted by Joe LeSueur, Frank's lover, very blond and beautiful; Joan Mitchell, with her impossibly thick and tinted glasses; and Norman Bluhm, his hooded eyes and the Gauloises hanging from his lip giving him the air of a gangster. At six or seven I felt especially grown up as I moved among them, and beamed when Frank announced that his drink was perfect. I always hurried through the meal when my mother called us in for supper, eager to get back to the adults. Carey quickly returned to her room, where she sometimes prayed to a small shrine for a return to normalcy.

Our block in those years had the feel of old New York, when neighborhoods were defined not so much by geographic boundaries as the people who inhabited them. Many of the men worked as longshoremen on the nearby piers, and almost everyone was Irish Catholic. A local kid named Jackie Hanley walked our German shepherds, Teufel and Gretel, and soon became a close friend. With a big belly and bright smile despite several missing teeth, Jackie was a unique presence. He was one of those rare personalities who seemed to be comfortable in any situation, a quality which, along with his humor and intelligence, helped him transcend the poverty and ignorance into which he was born. The only thing which seemed to unsettle him was the prospect of coming out of the closet, not surprising given his Catholic roots, and over the years our family provided a good deal of needed support.

Jackie and I took many long walks with the dogs. Sometimes we were gone for hours, roaming all over the Village, exploring the docks and even going down to the Battery and back in a blizzard. He seemed to know everyone on the street, and people occasionally fell into step as if under the spell of a Pied Piper. Five years older, Jackie was my big brother as well as my friend.

"Eleanor, come up for dinner!"

The command was hollered down every afternoon precisely at five, and it became the code with which Jackie and I would always call up our years on 11th Street. Barely audible above the din of children playing stickball or hopscotch, passing trucks, or the fruit vendor hawking his wares in broken English as his horse-drawn cart made its way west toward the river, the young girl invariably responded, "Okay, Ma! I'm coming!" After she ran inside, the "callous belly," as the watchful mothers were sometimes called, withdrew from the windowsill.

Jackie's brothers built a pigeon coop on our roof, maybe one of the last on the West Side, and I spent endless hours tending the birds or watching them swirl, roll, and dive while stretched out on the warm tar paper. I had my first sips of beer up there, at ten or eleven, but one day a callous belly saw what was going on and yelled at the Hanleys. After their mother was told, it didn't happen again. Nevertheless, that I'd been allowed to drink, even if only a little, was as exciting as the secrecy to which I was sworn. From the first swallow I believed this was something special, conferring on me a unique status which was as thrilling as the mild intoxication I usually experienced. Forced off the roof, my early dalliance with alcohol moved indoors.

"Here you go, Lukey," Sylvia said when I was twelve. "Take a sip, but not too much." More than housekeeper and babysitter, Sylvia was a family friend, and I loved her. The offer of scotch was always made surreptitiously, when no one else was around. We thought it was terrific, delighting in our shared transgression and the TV sitcoms she adored.

Besides hosting crowded fetes in our top-floor apartment, my mother was actively involved in the avant-garde literary world, contributing regularly to the *Evergreen Review*. She also translated books from French to English for Grove Press, working closely with Barney Rossett and Richard Seaver. Ironically, Dick had been on the staff of *Merlin* magazine when the communist periodical was the chief rival of the *Paris Review*. While the tall young men were headed for the literary mainstream, she was steering in precisely the opposite direction. Instead of Hemingway, the *Evergreen Review* crowd looked toward Beckett and the other modernists.

My mother bought her house on Old Stone Highway in 1961. With large oak beams traversing its ceiling, the living room had once been the den of an oceanfront mansion. That house was otherwise destroyed by the 1938 hurricane, but the den was trucked to Springs where less grand rooms were attached to it. A big multicolored abstraction of Mike's, five by seven feet, hung next to the bar.

Globs of oil paint stuck to its surface, some of which still hadn't dried after more than seven years. I always stopped to touch the largest when we returned in June, its perpetual tackiness somehow confirming that all was right in the world. Over the long shoeless days of summer this house came to feel like my real home. Aside from endless hours in the ocean, I loved the smell of warm earth and salt grass, the dogs lying in the shade, the late afternoon stillness, the faint mustiness of the blue canvas window seats, and Ray Charles singing "I Can't Stop Loving You" as the night came on.

The front door was always open, a string of Indian bells hanging on its inside, and guests were always welcome. My mother was usually dressed in a blue work shirt, open over a bathing suit. With her blonde hair and perennial tan, her cornflower blue eyes seemed to glow in the sunlight. Because she kept a horse at a nearby stable, Carey was often clad in riding gear, a black velvet hat highlighting the incipient elegance of her features. When not with friends we resumed our special connection, surfing the waves on our red and blue canvas rafts or playing Monopoly on rainy days.

The house in Springs was as much a gathering place for the bohemian scene as the apartment on 11th Street. Frank and Joe came out all the time, so much so that Carey named her first cat Joe the Pussy. My mother snapped a picture of my cat, Dotty Stein, sitting on Bill de Kooning's chest, both looking thoroughly content. Although the party continued unabated here, the atmosphere was calmer. Since the gatherings were generally held outdoors, perhaps the alcohol-induced clamor was diffused by the wind or absorbed in the trees.

I never stopped thinking of Mike as my stepfather, even after my mother divorced him in 1965. He moved into his studio on the Bowery—originally the basketball court of a YMCA— the following year, a space which would remain his home until his death in 2007. Mike had taken it over from Mark Rothko, and traces of Rothko red could still be seen on the floor. I always looked at the paintings as soon as I arrived, proud whenever my impressions of the work matched his ideas. Then I might hit the punching bag or climb his huge scaffold before we went out to lunch in Little Italy.

In the cruelest of ironies, Frank O'Hara was struck by a dune buggy on Fire Island, where no cars are allowed, in July 1966. He was buried a few days later in Green River Cemetery, about a quarter mile from our house in Springs. Jackson Pollock's headstone, an enormous boulder bearing his signature in bronze, sits thirty yards away. More than anyone else, Frank had sparked the remarkable collaboration between the painters and poets in the early sixties, and it seemed that the entire New York art crowd came out for his funeral. After his death, the sense of community and collective purpose he had inspired began to dissolve, and the world I had known changed forever. Everyone loved Frank, including me, but I was already armoring myself against grief. Riding the train back to New York not long after his burial, I jotted down a short poem, one of the few I have ever written. It ended with "Fuck you, Frank."

At the end of the following summer I carried a pair of garden shears to the cemetery. Frank's grave was covered with ivy and marked by a flat stone. "Grace to be born and live as variously as possible," a line from his poem "In Memory of My Feelings," had been chosen for his epitaph. The ivy had partially obscured the inscription, so I clipped it back before brushing off the dirt and bird shit. Although the day was hot, a breath of autumn chill was on the wind. The cicadas had gone silent, and a few dead leaves littered the lawn. Sitting cross-legged next to his headstone, I pledged to return every year.

If asked what was most memorable about growing up among the bohemians, I might first point to sitting with Mike and other abstract expressionists in the old Cedar Tavern on West Broadway, which still had sawdust on the floor in the early sixties; or driving around Springs at incredible speeds in Norman Bluhm's Citroën;

or, years later, drinking until dawn with Joan Mitchell. But then I would remember the tomato fights I had with Frank, always on the hottest afternoons. Once every summer we stopped at a farmers' market and picked up two baskets of the rottenest tomatoes we could find. Laughing as we tried to dodge our squishy missiles, Frank and I pelted each other silly. When we finally hosed down, the cold water was perfect.

My father's world was more subdued, so much so that going to visit him in those days was like abruptly switching from Ornette Coleman to Haydn. From the first, he was the defender of good manners, structured norms, and proper boundaries. But the time I spent with him, if more constrained on one level, was no less interesting. As far back as I can remember, he hoped to instill in me a passion not just for literature, but also nature and social justice.

Roughly ten miles west of Springs, Sagaponack was open country in the sixties. Most of its residents lived along the main street, which was lined with clusters of sycamore and maple. Bordered by the Atlantic, the Montauk Highway, Wainscott, and the village of Bridgehampton, its potato fields stretched almost unbroken from the highway to the ocean. Forty years before Wall Street tycoons snatched up much of the land, transforming the tiny hamlet into the wealthiest community in the country, nothing blocked the view from my father's house to the dunes.

Sagaponack always struck me as a more traditional place. It was tidier, more manicured, the most notable exception being the wild privet which rose to tree level around my father's property. Its houses and lawns were larger, and its children attended the Little Red Schoolhouse. With swings and seesaws out front, the first four grades were still taught in a single classroom by one Mrs. Grubb.

We had beach picnics in those early summers, the dunes sheltering us from the wind. As the sun went down we soaked the fresh-picked corn in seawater before throwing the ears, still in their husks, on the coals. My father's closest friend, Sherry Lord, was usually there with his wife, Cile, and Piedy and Peter Gimbel came with their two children, Bailey and Leslie. Piedy had been my father's first love, and they were still friends after more than twenty years. Listening to the slow rhythm of the surf as I sat wrapped in a towel before the fire, Sagaponack almost felt like home.

Unlike the wild abstractions coming out of Springs, Sherry painted delicate landscapes, firmly rooted in the Fairfield Porter tradition. The conversation, if not more refined, was definitely more restrained. Their banter was rarely punctuated with "fuck" or "shit," words which were always on everyone's lips in Springs, and things never got too raucous.

My father married Deborah Love in 1962. A socialite from St. Louis, she had beautiful almond eyes, a slight ball at the end of her nose, and a soft, warm laugh. She came with her daughter, Rue, four years old and a compact whirlwind of energy and pluck, and a son, Alex, would be born two years later. After the film rights to *At Play in the Fields of the Lord* were sold in 1965, Deborah oversaw extensive renovations to the house, including the conversion of the ground-floor garage into a spacious living room.

Because it eventually featured fossils, a meteorite, a few family antiques, and three of Sherry's paintings, one might have learned a great deal about my father by examining the decor. I always took a moment to look at the photographs he had taken in New Guinea. They showed tribesmen at war, some holding the same kind of spear which rested in brackets on the wall. My favorite was a portrait of a single warrior, shot from below, his head tilted toward the sky in open-mouthed joy. Crossing to the other side of the fireplace, I sought out the shrunken head my father had brought back from South America, nearly hidden in a shadowy corner. The unfortunate man's features were perfectly preserved under a dusty bell jar, the eyes sewn shut as if in sleep.

The movie sale also funded a celebratory trip to Ireland, and I was invited to come along. We set sail for Cobh on the RMS

Sylvania, a smaller sister in the Cunard fleet. I had a terrific time exploring the ship, and Deborah and my father were much amused by my twelve-year-old élan when I asked the waiter to send my compliments to the chef. Finally arriving at Lough Corrib, near the town of Headford in Galway, we settled into a house on a small island fifty yards from shore. It faced Annaghkeen, a ruined castle whose only tenants were several dairy cows. Like Ross Errily, a nearby medieval abbey, and the men walking the dirt roads in their rumpled coats and tweed caps, the castle seemed to be an ageless and permanent fixture of the land. We had come to a magical place, and hardly a day went by when Rue and I didn't row out on the lake, often pretending to be pirates on the high seas.

That summer my father presented me with a copy of *Twenty Years A' Growing*, a short autobiographical sketch of a young man's coming of age in rural Ireland. I finished it in one sitting before a peat fire on a rainy afternoon, a high wind raising small whitecaps on the lake. The story resonated with me, and its musical prose sparked a love of reading which, although it would remain dormant for several years, was perhaps his greatest gift.

A few months later it was decided that I should go to boarding school. At thirteen, I, too, was coming of age, and to "prep" was apparently part of my birthright. I had hoped to stay with my friends in the city, but instead joined four paternal cousins at St. Paul's in Concord, New Hampshire. I can still picture myself in those days—pudgy, sporting tortoiseshell glasses, acutely uncomfortable in the requisite gray flannels and blue blazer; alienation, confusion, and uncertainty were apparent in every aspect of my bearing. After two years I finally broke down, my stiff upper lip beginning to tremble before a rush of tears. When my father took me in his arms and assured me I wouldn't be returning in the fall, I had never felt so loved by him, cherishing a closeness I hadn't thought possible. In that moment it didn't matter that I probably wouldn't see him for another three months, that he would be far away and inaccessible while gathering material for his next book, or that I had allowed myself to blubber like a baby. Sitting together on the edge of my bed, it was safe to be honest, and safe to love him.

My father admired no one more than Cesar Chavez. He was especially excited before the publication of *Sal Si Puedes*, his book on Chavez and the Mexican farmworkers' boycott. A gifted racon-teur, he recounted anecdotes which reflected not only his deep respect for Chavez, his courage and modest leadership, but also the spirit of protest which Chavez and others had come to embody. By then Bob Dylan had bumped Mozart from the Sagaponack turnta-ble, and my father occasionally paused to sing along. I was proud that he had joined the ranks of those publicly questioning the status quo, years away from appreciating the extent to which guilt about his "unearned privilege," as he called it, would remain a driving force behind his commitment to be a voice for the disenfranchised.

We always took a walk to the beach when I visited. The potato fields stretched out on both sides of the road, from Bridge Lane down to Sag Pond and the dunes. Sometimes birds straddled the telephone wires. Starlings, he told me, pointing to a distant great blue heron. Scanning the pond's shore, I couldn't pick out the heron until he raised his long neck from the water.

My father was fully present when we were outdoors, most giving when he saw something—a rare bird, mussels clinging to a pier, a horseshoe crab inching its way toward the water—which he hoped might ignite a shared enthusiasm. He delighted in explaining the simple anatomy of a clam, or happening upon a bird's nest with speckled eggs inside.

He had first been tutored on the workings of nature by his par-ents, and carried on that tradition whenever we visited them. "Caw, caw, caw," he called, the sound reverberating through the woods behind my grandparents' Connecticut house. At five and four, Carey and I stood transfixed, waiting in patient silence for the crows to come. After a pause he raised his hands and called again, and it was only a few seconds before we heard the far-off reply. We whooped with delight as he turned to us, allowing himself a brief but proud smile.

Trips to Fishers Island, where my grandparents had their summer house, were always centered around boats. Perched on the prow of the "Echo," Carey and I sat spellbound as we entered the turbulent waters of the Race, where Long Island Sound meets the Atlantic. But the best ship of all was no more than five feet long. A tiny gray rowboat just big enough for two children, it was kept on the beach below the house. We rowed out into the small inlet and pretended to be adrift on the ocean, taking care not to venture beyond the protective promontories on either side.

Well before their deaths, my parents had attained an almost mythical stature. Their lives have been repeatedly chronicled over the years, and both held up as paragons of their era. My mother was the belle of the downtown scene in the sixties, the witty, funny, and beautiful Patsy, whom all the straight artists and writers wanted to sleep with, and all the gay ones adored. Until her life was nearly over, she never stopped rebelling, experimenting, thumbing her nose at the status quo whenever she could. Passing a golf course one afternoon when in her sixties, she leaned out the car window and yelled to a man in lime-green pants, "Fore, asshole!"

Although he would maintain his detachment from the politics and social mores of his birth, my father would always strive for the highest recognition from the literary establishment. He was the lion of the "Sag Main" crowd, the writer whose evocative prose masked a deeply competitive and sometimes intimidating nature, the National Book Award winner who did as much as anyone to popularize Zen Buddhism in the seventies and eighties.

Even as a child I knew I was surrounded by special people doing special things. They were making art, and I understood this to be the most important thing one could do, a sentiment which would dictate much of my life over the next thirty years. Too young to appreciate the cultural significance of their work, I saw their names on books, in galleries and magazines. Their energy—and, in some cases, genius—was palpable, and I was a young kid in the middle of it. The magazines and books tended to idealize almost everything about my two worlds, and so did I. But could I ever measure up?

To a young child, the parents are four times larger, make all the rules, provide food, clothing, and shelter, and dispense both love and punishment. But what if those gods are a little crazy? What if they go away, get drunk regularly, suddenly become irrational and otherwise appear to lose control? Such behavior might well suggest that the whole universe is unpredictable and chaotic, a terrifying vision to a little kid. But if he unconsciously assumes himself to be the cause of their misdoings, as I have seen countless times over the course of my work, isn't the infallibility of the gods—and the stability of the outside world—ultimately preserved? The psychological cost ("It's my fault," "I must not be good enough") is enormous, but it is almost universally preferable to the alternative.

I have always believed that I was brought up by loving parents who did the best they could to provide their children with a good home. That said, throughout much of my early life I continued to see the adults I grew up with through a rosy lens, much as the journalists did, almost refusing to look at anything but a glossier version of events. But that was never the whole story.

Paris was not a carefree literary romp for my parents. Their first son was born prematurely and died a few days later. Both resisted speaking to me about their shared tragedy, making it plain that this was territory best left undisturbed. Some reports have it that the boy was to be called Thomas, but I never heard this from either of them. That my father was also a covert operative for the CIA while in France wasn't known until many years after our return. When they learned of it, both Doc Humes and George Plimpton were infuriated by his duplicity.

My mother's love of everything French—and lifelong disdain of my grandmother, a Michigan socialite—probably started on the morning she came downstairs at age six to find that her French governess, whom she adored, had been peremptorily dismissed. I can only imagine how excited she must have been, a young woman right out of college, at the prospect of starting a new life on the Seine. But while my father was busy founding the *Paris Review* and working on his first novel, she wasn't having quite so good a time of it. She described herself in Talese's article as a "Stepin Fetchit" for the men, and told me years later that all she ever did was make sandwiches. She felt she had been relegated to the role of the artist's wife, much like Lee Krasner to Jackson Pollock, so it was only natural that they later became friends.

My father ended their marriage after learning of my mother's affair with a neighbor, a journalist named Jeffrey Potter, who had an affected English accent and the most rigid posture I have ever seen. Although neither spoke at any length about the circumstances behind their breakup, my mother once confided that Potter, with whom she would take up again, always loved her. After her death in 1998 my father confessed to his own infidelity as we walked along a windy winter beach. I don't believe she knew of his trysts, since she wouldn't have been able to contain her outrage over such hypocrisy, but something had badly wounded her. In any case, their separate camps would always be incompatible, at odds, impossible to reconcile.

The decadence of bohemian life had its price. In 1961, on the anniversary of her husband's death, Lee Krasner asked me, "Will you stay with me tonight, Lulu?" Pollock died after drunkenly steering into a tree near our Springs house in 1956, and she always needed company on that night. I agreed and, perhaps surprising for an eight-year-old, didn't take offense at being called "Lulu."

At least once every summer in the early sixties Carey and I saw a white-haired man coming toward us on his bicycle, his eyes angry and fixed on the road. As he drew nearer we lifted our hands in greeting. "Hello, Mr. de Kooning," we sang out, but his stern countenance betrayed no recognition or acknowledgment, and he didn't speak. He rode slowly, stiffly, his hands rigid on the handlebars, and I wondered how he managed to remain upright. We knew he was drinking again, and my mother or some other friend would soon take him to the hospital.

Mike, too, was hospitalized in 1965, but for much longer than a five-day detox. When no real explanation was given for his sudden removal to a psych ward, I began to curl in on myself, snarling like a wounded animal whenever anyone got too close. All he would say when we went to visit was that the whole thing was "kind of silly" and promised to come home soon. Like the bright yellows and reds of the hospital's dayroom, or the sunlight streaming through its oversized windows, this did little to mitigate my fear and confusion. Three years later my mother finally revealed that, along with forging her checks, he had stolen several paintings from de Kooning's studio. Carey and I had always suspected that Mike had robbed our piggy banks, but this was different, wrapped in a scary aura of serious crime and mental illness.

She went on to say that a meeting had been set up between the FBI, the purchasers of the paintings (Chicago-based mobsters, I was told), and de Kooning's attorney at a jukebox distribution center on the Lower East Side. My mother's lawyer was able to broker a deal which satisfied all parties and kept Mike out of prison. If the money and paintings were returned, Bill agreed not to press charges and the FBI agreed to Mike's entering a psychiatric institution for one year in lieu of jail time. My mother filed for divorce and sold the 11th Street house shortly thereafter. She would always love Mike, his energy and humor, but in the end just couldn't deal with his craziness.

While I still look back on my childhood as some of the happiest years of my life, I didn't always approve of my mother's behavior. A soprano in the choir of my Episcopalian grammar school, I was careful that none of my friends was around when there was a gathering of people they might think weird or "faggy." One day, brimming with seven-year-old moral indignation, I called her a "beatnik nudist" as she stood topless before the bathroom mirror, and she smiled lovingly. We had a good laugh over that exchange in later years, but some of what went on will never be funny. For example, I knew how to mix a Bloody Mary before I was out of the first grade. That this was sanctioned and even encouraged by the adults around me is today a little frightening, not least because it gave me such a thrill to do it.

One night Carey and I were alone on 11th Street, waiting for Sylvia to get back from Springs. Someone called to say that she had been in an accident nearby. It was close to ten, and I told Carey I would return soon. I arrived at the scene to find Sylvia dead drunk and our car wrapped around a lamppost. After everything was straightened out, I walked her back to our house and put her to bed, proud that I had handled the situation like an adult. Since Sylvia remained with us, my mother apparently concluded that her love of scotch wasn't a high crime, or even much of a misdemeanor.

Just as it was hard for some to admit that Frank had probably been drinking before he was struck on Fire Island, I was nearly forty before I could accept that it wasn't all just fun. Until then I had seen the probability that most of Frank's lunch poems were written with a bad hangover as an amusing footnote, unaware or unwilling to acknowledge that this might have been a sign of a serious problem.

Upon hearing that he had been gravely injured, my mother wept in great bursts and rushed to the hospital. She drank heavily, unable to sit still or be comforted. When not by his side she was on the phone, getting the updates which eventually confirmed that he wouldn't survive. After his death she withdrew to her bedroom, drink in hand. Her brief remembrance, "My Night with Frank

O'Hara," hints that he was not just her best friend, but perhaps the great unrequited love of her life.

On the day of his funeral we walked from our house to the cemetery. The afternoon was sunny and hot, perfect for a tomato fight, but there wasn't enough room for everyone in the shade of the tree near Frank's grave. In an effort to drive home the full reality of his death to the scores who had come seeking solace and understanding, Larry Rivers, sometimes considered the first pop artist and Frank's occasional lover and collaborator, described the purplish color of Frank's skin, the swelling, the many sutures, his rapid, shallow breathing, and the perpetual quivering of his entire frame. Several people interrupted, pleading with him to stop, but Rivers went on. "In the crib he looked like a shaped wound, an innocent victim of someone else's war." Like many others, I stood dazed, uncomprehending.

Afterward the assembled walked to our house, and everyone attempted to console themselves and each other as best they could, many by getting very drunk. Carey and I were shielded from Lafcadio Orlovsky masturbating between two slices of bread. The brother of Allen Ginsberg's lover, Peter, Lafcadio had recently been released from a mental hospital. The godfather of the Beat poets chanted throughout the afternoon in his Buddhist regalia.

"I loved him so much. I loved him so much," Joe LeSueur wailed. Racked by gut-wrenching sobs, he declared his undying devotion to everyone, sometimes grabbing on to friends to steady himself. It was a display of grief the likes of which I wouldn't see for another thirty years.

My mother's drinking started to become a problem after she separated from Mike, roughly a year before Frank's death, and others began to worry about my sister's and my welfare. Unbeknownst to us, my father decided that salubrious alternatives to spending another summer in Springs had to be found. To that end, I was taken to Ireland, and my sister, already a second-class citizen in the family hierarchy, was packed off to a camp in Vermont. A year later my mother's drinking had worsened to the point where he felt the need to intervene for a second time. Once again, it would be several years before I learned that I was sent to St. Paul's not so much in observance of family tradition, but more to remove me from the chaos. Things were apparently so bad that even Frank assisted in my transition to boarding school, writing a letter of recommendation which, while laudatory, also noted that I tended to be too "idealistic." When I headed up to New Hampshire, Carey moved out to Sagaponack.

Thanks to the marvelous powers of repression, I have no memory of my mother's drunkenness in those years. Although I disliked prep school intensely, anxiety about the turmoil at home doubtlessly fueled my desire to get back to New York. I had been similarly sullen in Ireland the year before, and my father finally presented me with the choice of improving my attitude or flying home at once. The ultimatum was delivered as we sat together on a stone fence, and it is the only distinct memory I have of being with him. Not wishing to be a quitter, I chose to stick it out.

Almost every portrait of my father references his patrician background. No matter how much he attempted to distance himself, his bearing and accent betrayed his upbringing. But while the plight of brown-skinned peoples would remain a primary focus of his nonfiction, his friends were almost uniformly wealthy and white. He liked being in the company of celebrities even before he achieved his own share of notoriety, and it wasn't uncommon for a Kennedy or two to show up at his Sunday afternoon touch football games. In the end, despite his conversion to Zen and dedication to being a voice for the marginalized victims of corporate greed, he would never stray too far from a kind of bohemian gentility. Perhaps confirming Frank's assessment of excessive idealism, I felt a twinge of disappointment when I could no longer deny that side of him.

As a young child I first began to appreciate that I had been born into wealth when visiting my grandparents. They kept servants, belonged to the local clubs, had a sixty-five-foot yacht and were otherwise fully representative of their upper-class WASP communities. They were invariably well-mannered and dignified, no matter how many cocktails were politely consumed.

With the exception of a delicately beautiful line drawing of my grandmother above the mantel in Stamford, one which revealed an inner fragility she otherwise never showed, their homes were decorated in the prescribed style of the old-money gentry. Aside from one or two family photographs, there were few personal touches—my grandmother's shell collection in a glass-topped coffee table, or my grandfather's duck decoys on a shelf off the front hallway—and nothing was ever out of place. Children were expected to be presentable at all times, and Carey and I were regularly sent back to our room to wash our hands or change our muddy clothes.

We couldn't articulate it when we were small, but my sister and I sensed that our grandparents had designated us as the black sheep of our generation. Not surprising, since my father had fulfilled that role before us. Unlike our cousins, we didn't live in proper New England homes, and we were the children of divorce. Instead of wool cardigans and khakis, we were almost always clad in jeans and hooded sweatshirts. In some ways we felt like ugly ducklings, a little pitied and occasionally a cause for embarrassment

Even though they had once been close, my grandfather never spoke of his cousin, F. O. Matthiessen. On the few occasions his name came up he kept silent, his features assuming a hardness I didn't often see. Although I wouldn't learn the circumstances behind F. O'.s suicide until I met with Trilling, at fifteen I could imagine how his homosexuality and bookish tendencies must have been greeted by an earlier generation of German American industrialists. That he had gone on to become one of the foremost experts on Henry and William James probably hadn't counted for much.

I remember my father hitting me only once, when he found me at age eight threatening to throw a brick at Carey, who had picked up a log. But while he came to her rescue on that occasion, she would rarely feel protected or understood by him, and had anything but a good time while living in Sagaponack. Eventually growing into the rebel of our generation, she fought bitterly with my father, demanding the kind of attention he just couldn't deliver. That dynamic would play out again and again over the next three decades, and both became progressively frustrated by their inability to reach the other. When she gradually lapsed into serious depression in her late thirties, any hope that they might one day sustain a loving relationship slowly faded into mutual fantasy.

Since he traveled a good deal and I didn't see him often, it was usually on our walks that I reconnected with my father. Even if it didn't always feel quite natural, I gave him my news and he offered paternal counsel. He never failed to excite my interest when I was with him, and most of what he showed me was fascinating. But while he always stressed the importance of being curious, no matter the subject, I sensed from an early age that he would much prefer it if my interests mirrored his.

Along with the relics of his travels and good times out on the water, I remember the quiet, and how the Sagaponack house was always cold in winter. I don't recall playing there as a child, but I remember waiting. By the end of a meal his gaze was usually elsewhere, out into the distance. After breakfast I often watched as he walked out to his studio, head down, wearing corduroy jeans and moccasins.

I experienced wonderful things when I was young, traveling to more places before my sixteenth birthday than many will see in a lifetime. Exposed to great music, art, and literature, I came to know some of the most interesting people of that era. Always encouraged to shun conformity, I grew up in a vortex of creativity and diverse passions. Nevertheless, I sometimes shared my sister's desire for "normalcy," occasionally fantasizing about being renamed Bob Smith and having a father who returned every night on the 6:23.

Four

ALCOHOLICS NEVER KNOW EXACTLY HOW OR WHY THEY BECAME alcoholic. Most theories point to genetic or environmental causes, or a combination of the two. My history would seem to reinforce both, since I can trace the problem back for at least two generations on my mother's side, and then there were the heavy drinkers who shaped my early life. On the other hand, I know plenty of people who grew up in similar circumstances who did not become alcoholic.

Researchers have more recently identified trauma as a major catalyst for addiction, and there is plenty of good science to support that theory. But while it has both physical and emotional components, the importance of another element, what is sometimes referred to as the "spiritual" dimension, is too often underestimated. When all the hypotheses are stripped away, a central truth remains: people drink to change the way they feel. This was the essence of my alcoholism, and the need to understand the full extent of that reality and all it implied was ultimately as important to my recovery as abstinence.

At fifteen I had no concept of spirituality beyond the standard dogma of the Judeo-Christian tradition, or the counterculture alternatives proffered by the flower children of the sixties. It was either swallowing the teachings of the Episcopalian church or donning a string of beads over a tie-dye shirt. Because neither called to me, I rejected their promises of inner peace and salvation. Further, I had no inkling that what was ailing me—a pervasive sense of low self-esteem, of being "less than" other people—might be, at its core, a spiritual malaise. "Spiritual" was something nebulous, abstract, elusive, of no discernible use, heady stuff for ministers and hippies, but not me.

After my father took up Zen Buddhism, I was even less inclined to pursue a spiritual path, intuitively wary of drawing nearer or following his lead. It would be many years before I began to realize that I would need to "go in," a prospect which, even in recovery, filled me with dread. Eventually, like so many others, I would learn that I had little choice if I hoped to stay sober.

In my adolescence, alcohol seemed to have transformational powers which I wanted to experience as often as possible. After a few drinks I felt adequately intelligent, funny, social, sexual, and otherwise on a par with everyone else. It was the magical elixir that helped me feel comfortable in the world, a sensation for which I would eventually sacrifice almost anything. I continued to have faith in alcohol's divine properties long after these had vanished, desperately hoping to retrieve the deceptive contentment of its spell.

As a child I sensed that alcohol made life more exciting. At cocktail time the adults became loquacious and playful, vibrant and alive. I heard the music and laughter, saw the smiles and camaraderie, and loved the smell of gin, whiskey, and French cigarettes. Not just the people, it was alcohol which made the parties so special, even if things did get out of hand from time to time.

One weekend when I was six or seven Carey and I went with my father to visit his old friend William Styron. In the Connecticut autumn, the leaves were beginning to turn the luminous yellows and reds rarely seen on Long Island. We played with the Styron kids next to a secluded pool across the road from their house. Approached by a path through the woods, I pretended we were in a special place made just for children. That night, drunk as a lord, Bill climbed on a coffee table and, with Chubby Checker blaring in the background, shouted to the heavens, "All we do in this house is twist and fuck." I was spellbound but also frightened, unsure whether everything was really all right. Looking back, I sometimes wonder that early experiences like this didn't scare me off booze forever. But from my first drink I chose not to see alcohol's darker side, oblivious to everything but its charms.

My father made good on his promise to pull me out of St. Paul's, and I transferred to the Solebury School in New Hope, Pennsylvania, in the fall of 1968. As relieved as I was to have escaped the strictures of St. Paul's, it was clear that adjusting to Solebury would take some time. Jackets, ties, and Gothic arches were nowhere to be found, and there were no other outward signs of prestige, grandeur, or wealth. Cornfields abutted the small campus on two sides, and the fecund aromas of late summer suffused the air.

Someone knocked as I was unpacking. Identical twins with fiery red hair and eyes nearly shut stood in the hallway. Clad in bell-bottoms, they looked as if they had just stepped out of Robert Crumb's Zap Comix. One held a pipe made of small brass plumbing fixtures, and the other asked for a match. They moved almost imperceptibly, something between a jiggle and a bop, and both began to giggle. Stepping inside, they lit up on the spot. Because I had gone at least a hundred yards into the woods to smoke a cigarette at St. Paul's, I was astounded by their lack of concern.

One introduced himself as Jeff and identified his brother, who was drawing heavily on the pipe, as John. I replied that it was nice to meet them, and they broke into identical peals of laughter. Pleasantly sweet smoke erupted from John's nose and mouth.

They offered me the pipe but I declined, beginning to feel a little self-conscious in my button-down shirt.

The composition of Solebury's boarding students was changing with the times. Quite a few had been previously enrolled in other institutions. Like me, some had chosen to leave their prep schools, while others had been thrown out of them. With the instincts of a homing pigeon, I sought out those who liked to drink and get high. Jeff and John were from New York. Despite my initial awkwardness, I was drawn to them, the first real hippies I had ever met. They somehow managed to incorporate the word "man" in almost every sentence, speaking with an unaffected ease which soon helped me shake off the residual inhibitions of my St. Paul's days.

Michael was a black kid from the East Village projects whose speech often echoed that of his Puerto Rican neighbors. Michael spoke not just with words, but with his hands and head, body gestures, and innumerable inflections. For Michael, communication was about movement, and he always seemed to be on the verge of dancing to an inner rhythm. He was funny, loyal, smart, streetwise and, like Jackie, completely relaxed in everyone's company. It wasn't long before I was adopting some of his not-too-Castilian Spanish whenever we were together.

Steven, also from New York, rounded out the core quartet of my first-year friends. Like Jeff and John, Steven was a full-fledged hippie, skinny and with hair past his shoulders. He painted mandalas, listened to Captain Beefheart, and had an inquiring mind and a deep appreciation of art. I would later learn that he also possessed a keen aptitude for business, as yet untapped. Like the others, Steven loved to smoke pot.

Before the year was far advanced, I, too, was getting stoned. "Jamatao," as Michael called it, with red eyes and a broad smile. Only on weekends at first, since I hoped to do well academically, and always at night, away from the prying eyes of the school's faculty. Sometimes we went out to the "commando trail," a path through the surrounding woods with almost impenetrable flora. One evening I couldn't see the way and stumbled over a root before falling into a bramble patch. Jeff laughed affectionately and asked whether I'd been tippling.

I laughed, too, hoping the aromatic smoke would relax the knot in my stomach.

Although I didn't get high more than twice a week in that first year, my chemical horizons gradually expanded from marijuana, hashish, and cheap wine to include hallucinogens, barbiturates, and, eventually, anything else I could get my hands on. Like my friends, I never suspected that there might be serious consequences to using. I was doing well, so there was no cause for concern.

Before year's end the principles of openness and freedom at the core of the school's approach to learning had been not just tested, but essentially corrupted. The onslaught of the sixties had caught the administration off guard, and they had no idea how to contain so many young people hell-bent on getting high and having a good time. We cared little for the school's authority, since it was obvious that about the only way to get thrown out was to be caught red-handed by the police with a needle in your arm, and even then there was a good chance of talking your way out of it.

Shortly before classes ended one of the English teachers rode off with a female student on the back of his motorcycle, leaving a wife and three children behind. A male student began an affair with the school nurse. I went one weekend to New York with Anton, another friend, where we bought a C-melody sax in a pawn shop on Third Avenue. Hurrying back to school with our prize, we got drunk before climbing to the roof of a shed near the football field. It was after midnight when we began taking turns playing the horn, passing a fifth of bourbon back and forth. A bearded math teacher with hair longer than that of any student came out, his guitar in hand. We jammed for fifteen minutes before the head-master arrived and asked us to shut it down.

My father's words in the Land Rover had come back to me throughout the year, quiet but persistent, like the far-off ringing of a ship's bell on a foggy night. Certain I would find my muse at Solebury, I pledged early on to tell him of my commitment to pursue my place in the Matthiessen trinity, but by summer had neither sent that letter nor written a single word. He never pressured me, his silence almost audible as I waited for inspiration to come.

Many people in recovery believe they stopped growing emotionally when they crossed the line into addiction. At sixteen I was preparing for my future vocation not with the disciplined forethought of my father, but with what those in my field refer to as the "magical thinking" often seen in young children—the belief that, if I wish it, it will happen. That I might need to study the craft never occurred to me. Further, it never crossed my mind that I would need to write and write and write in order to write. On some level I believed that writing would just come to me, and all I had to do on that day was take my seat. I don't recall whether I attempted to excuse my drinking as an essential part of becoming a real artist, like Frank or Mike, but probably would have if I'd thought of it.

Eager for new discoveries, I returned to Springs. Every day held the potential for something exciting or sensual, a fantasy realized or a new vista suddenly opening. Riding the wave of that extraordinary time, I was coming of age when anything seemed possible. Mike's painting was still wet, my mother's drinking was back under control, and the house was alive again.

Inspired by this sense of limitless opportunity, I decided to tell my mother about my father's declaration the previous summer. I'd thought it best not to say anything until her spirits revived, reluctant to invite the sardonic response which usually followed any mention of his name. We sat together on the deck, in blue and orange butterfly chairs, sharing an ashtray as we sipped our coffee.

Dressed in shorts and a faded *Paris Review* T-shirt, she astonished me by commending both the idea and my father for having suggested it. She was excited, playful, and loving, embracing her life again. When I confessed that I still hadn't put pen to paper, she reassured me that there was plenty of time and stressed that it was essential to read as much as possible to nurture my literary "voice." Incredibly, it had never occurred to me that reading might also be crucial to becoming a writer.

As if to celebrate the restoration of color to her life, my mother decided to host a large party, the first since Frank's funeral. The day was unusually hot for June, and I sweated heavily as I mowed the lawn and set up the bar under a three-story birdhouse, a tenement for sparrows. The bar had always been in that spot, and I saw no reason to change things now.

Looking over a last-minute shopping list, my mother asked me to bring her a pen from the dining room table Mike had made. Covered with four-inch-square Mexican tiles—blue, gold, and white—the top rested on an ornate iron stand, spray painted yellow. Lee Krasner's "Ode to Mr. Blue," an homage to Frank, hung on the wall behind it. I scanned the table but couldn't see the pen, and told her so.

Turning to look, she said it was right there, right in front of me. Didn't I see it? Was there something wrong? She sounded more confused than annoyed, as if she couldn't make sense of what was happening. Still looking, I began to apologize when I finally saw the pen and brought it to her.

Like Jeff, she wondered whether I'd been drinking or using anything else, but I had not. After a pause she said she had seen me trip over a chair earlier that day, holding my gaze with her concern. Anxious to end the discussion, I confessed to occasional problems with my vision and agreed to see an eye doctor before retreating to my room.

A boxed edition of *The Brothers Karamazov* stood on a shelf, alongside books about baseball, sharks, and various school texts, but I felt no compulsion to read it. My mother's interrogation didn't seem fair, but I had been put on notice and knew I needed to be careful. Years later I would smile at the irony of being confronted when actually cold-stone sober, but not then. That morning I was more concerned with protecting my drinking than a possible problem with my eyesight, something which would make perfect sense to any alcoholic.

Dozens of people came that evening, mostly the Springs artists and their spouses, but also a number of poets, writers, and critics. But even the energy of the late sixties couldn't charge the evening like the exuberance of Frank and Mike, however much that had been fueled by gin. The relative tameness of this gathering was such that Carey judged it safe to socialize with the adults, a rarity in our younger days. I surreptitiously nursed a drink of my own as I tended bar, topping off whenever the plastic glass was less than half full.

We said goodbye to the last guests as night was coming on. I was glad the party had gone well, that my mother hadn't gotten too drunk or made a scene, and neither had I. This was the first time I served as a kind of cohost to her. Although she had a lover, a psychiatrist named Wayne Barker, she didn't often socialize with him. Nicknamed "Dr. Dogbreath," he had once been her therapist and was disliked by many, including me. One night at dinner he boasted that he was the only man who had ever brought her to orgasm, pressuring her to confirm this in my presence. Outraged and emboldened by a few cans of courage, I demanded that he apologize. She begged me to back down, on the verge of tears. When he refused and asked what I intended to do about it, I got up and grabbed the Masai spear I had brought back from Africa. Not sure whether I really meant business, he left the house. They remained together for another two years, but I had little to do with him and wasn't sorry to see him go.

My mother and I had always been close, even through the worst of her drinking, but that year marked the beginnings of a shift. She had started to treat me like a peer as much as a son, and I sometimes accompanied her to parties. By that time I was regularly offered a drink and took this as a sure sign that I was growing into manhood. Deaf to the off-stage whisperings of Sophocles and the good doctor Freud, I didn't see anything untoward about our relationship, thinking only that I was lucky to be included in the sphere of so many hip adults.

Later that summer, I traveled to Provincetown and Stockbridge with Mike and his girlfriend, a theatrical producer who was staging two plays. The first was Leonard Melfi's *The Jones Man*, which featured Fox Harris in the title role. Mike did the sets, essentially a lot of yellow feathers to simulate a beach, and I helped out as a stagehand wherever needed.

A party was held on opening night, and I began belting down shots of vodka, Dylan Thomas–style. The next thing I knew I was in bed with Stephanie, another stagehand, in flagrante delicto. I came out of my first blackout almost at the moment of orgasm, with no idea of what had happened over the previous hour or how I had ended up with dear Stephanie. Momentarily unnerved by the blackout phenomenon, my bewilderment was soon displaced by elation and wonder at having at last cleared the final hurdle of adolescent sexuality.

In Stockbridge we put on Patricia Cooper's *Short Play*, a harrowing dialogue between a single man on stage and an unseen voice. The voice was played by Richard Lynch, at the time the only person who had ever set himself on fire and survived. He had done it in Central Park after being up for two days on acid, and the resultant scarring would later make him a staple of horror films. Richard and I watched the first lunar landing together, and it was hard to tell which of us was more excited and amazed. Stoned on some excellent pot, we jumped out of our seats and hugged one another as Neil Armstrong bounced across the surface of the moon.

Jackie came out to Springs when I returned from Massachusetts. We spent most nights in the local bars and, after closing, often fished until dawn. As we sat on the dock with a six-pack, Jackie described the flight of bats chasing our lures. Everything felt right as I savored the smells of the harbor with my best friend, listening to channel buoys and halyards clanging against their masts. It didn't matter that I couldn't see the bats.

Carey joined me at Solebury when I returned for my junior year. For the first few weeks she seemed to be adjusting well, but it wasn't long before she was getting into verbal skirmishes with both students and faculty. When she was called into the assistant headmaster's office and told to "shape up or ship out," she opted to ship out on the spot. Unable to change her mind, I couldn't shake a conviction that things might have turned out differently had I been paying more attention, been more of a big brother.

In hindsight I see that I had essentially abandoned her years earlier. Despite being so close as young children, I had drifted away, leaving her to fend for herself in a family she often saw as alien and even hostile. By now possessed of a sharp tongue and keen intellect, she would soon earn the sobriquet of "Scary," but at the time I failed to see the hurt and loneliness beneath her tough exterior. This is not to say that she wasn't difficult, but perhaps more understanding and compassion might have alleviated her suspicion that no one really cared.

I was now smoking pot almost daily with Michael and Jeff, my new roommates. One night John, extremely stoned, astounded all of us by performing a fire-breathing dragon act with a tank of propane. Jeff brought back a pound of hash from the city, the perfect accompaniment to *Naked Lunch*, perhaps the only book I actually finished that year.

The following summer my mother agreed to let Steven and me stay in her Bank Street apartment. We insisted on paying the rent, and I assured her that this would be covered by the profits from our joint enterprise, People's Painters ("Old World Craftsmanship, New World Consciousness"), a venture we had launched the previous year. But instead of house painting we began dealing drugs on a large scale. Stoned-out and naive teenagers, we exercised almost no caution and gave no thought to the possibility that we might be placing ourselves in real danger.

Marijuana was our chief commodity, but we dispensed almost everything except amphetamines. Believing these had bad karma, we couldn't sell them in good conscience. At one point we had over a hundred pounds of pot on hand, which was delivered in ten-gallon paint cans and sold at a one-pound minimum. We thought ourselves quite the young entrepreneurs, and customers came and went at all hours of the night.

True to the spirit of the age, Steven and I also volunteered for the Black Panther Party and saw no conflict between this and how we were making our living. Initially amused by us, the Panthers were nonetheless grateful for our interest and enthusiasm. We showed up every day at the district office near Union Square and collected a card table, literature, and buttons featuring the great logo. We spread the word with dedication and absolute conviction in the rightness of the cause, impassioned social activists by day and ethical drug dealers by night.

"You need to get out of there right now. I mean it, Luke. Right now." I had never heard Jackie sound so alarmed, so urgent.

"I'm calling from a pay phone. Don't say anything. I was just at a party at my mother's. An off-duty cop is there shooting off his mouth. He's drunk and bragging about how they're going to get those two kids on Bank Street. He said the place is staked out, the phone tapped, and they've got everything they need to bust you. Get out now, please," he said, and hung up.

Terrified, we stayed just long enough to flush the harder—and more incriminating—stuff down the toilet, grabbed some clothes, and headed for Penn Station. Laying low in Springs for a few weeks before going back late one night to retrieve the marijuana, we never saw the apartment again.

While hiding out I went to a party where I was told that one of the guests was an especially gifted palm reader. She was drunk, but I was curious and asked her to look at my palm. Within a few seconds she closed my hand and began to weep.

"What's wrong?" I asked. "What did you see?"

"I can't tell you. It's too sad. I can't tell you," she said, and quickly left the room. Shaken, I longed to know why she had fled, but didn't pursue her then or later. Like many other nights that summer, I drove home too fast, too drunk, and realized again that I was having difficulty seeing the road.

Marijuana was beginning to make me too paranoid, and I couldn't "trip" as often as I would've liked. It just took too much out of me. As if to celebrate alcohol's final victory over all other contenders, I finished a fifth of bourbon in one sitting early in my senior year. Proud of it, I had no idea what benchmark this actually represented.

Two other relationships took shape at that time, their significance extending well beyond my graduation. Jonathan Becker had the slight build of his mother, a Martha Graham protégé, and also lived in New York. His father, the head of Janus Films, knew mine through George Plimpton. Jonathan lived uptown, which was probably why we had never met, but he, too, hadn't flourished in a traditional prep school. Although he outwardly championed the social mores of Southampton and the Upper East Side, Jonathan was never society's poster boy. Both of us took photographs, smoked unfiltered cigarettes, drank whisky, and understood the importance of close friendship. We had many adventures at school, some of which involved "borrowing" a faculty car or school bus.

Karen Andes was a day student, three years my junior. More beautiful than girlishly pretty, she was mature beyond her years and secure in herself, so I never had the feeling that I might be "robbing the cradle" or otherwise taking unfair advantage of an unsuspecting and innocent country girl. I gave her my heart and couldn't imagine being happier with anyone else.

My acceptance at Columbia was nothing short of miraculous. Not only had I taken the SATs on acid, I had also spilled coffee all over the application. When I arrived for my interview in Morningside Heights, the English teacher who had carried off the girl on his motorcycle sat behind the admissions desk. He asked why I wanted to come to a "hellish" place like Columbia, and I couldn't think of anything to say other than that it was in New York and an excellent school. We briefly discussed his woes before he said he would put in a good word, hoping this might offset my relatively low math score. Smiling as we shook hands at the door, he commended me for having had the guts to submit such a soiled pile of paper.

Shortly after graduation I drove to the Strong Insurance Agency in East Hampton to get coverage on the car my parents had given me. The broker, an older woman with dyed red hair and enormous glasses, had just started to review my application when she looked up and asked whether I was the one who crashed into the post office. Astonished by her memory and fearing that my premium had just doubled, I pleaded for clemency. Laughing, she promised not to hold my past against me, and I assured her that I was now a fully upstanding citizen. In less than half an hour I had bound myself to the terms of adult accountability, ready or not.

Karen came to Springs that summer, my mother relinquishing her bedroom for us. Such cohabitation never would have been permitted in my father's house, and he surely wouldn't have given up his bedroom. I took her to a local gynecologist named Dr. Fear, who reluctantly supplied her with birth control pills, and we couldn't see any further obstacles to our happiness.

Karen got a job in a local boutique, and I began working for Ted Lester, making deliveries and stocking shelves at the liquor store

he opened after retiring from fishing. With white hair and features heavily creased by a life on the water, Ted had once been the
patriarch of the local baymen. My father had worked on his haul
seining crew years earlier so, in one sense, I really was following in
his footsteps. On those afternoons when his wife didn't arrive with
a pitcher of highballs, Ted took me in the back room and poured
each of us a cup of cherry brandy, his favorite, and maybe an extra
one for good measure. It promised to be a terrific summer.

Late one afternoon my mother met me in the hall as I came
out of the bedroom. Karen was inside, dressing after her shower.
"There's something I've been meaning to ask you," she said.
"Would now be a good time?"

"Sure, Mom," I replied.

"You may have heard of it, but there's a new film called *Murmur
of the Heart* that I'd like to see, and maybe you'd like to see it with
me?"

"Sure," I said. "Tell me about it."

"Well," she said, looking straight at me and beginning to smile,
"it's about an affair between a mother and son. I hear it's very well
done."

I looked past her for a moment, my gaze scanning the large living room. In the silence which followed, broken only by her muted
giggle, I stared out the open front door toward the woods beyond.
Karen closed a drawer.

"Mom," I began, "I—"

"You know, I've always had a vision of how I would decorate
your bedroom. I'd have lots of embroidered pillows and silks hanging from the walls—"

"Mom," I interrupted. "I, well, I really don't . . ."

"Are you shocked?" she asked. "I hope not. It isn't so unusual,
you know, so unnatural." She was still smiling, an expression
which seemed to dare me with lascivious challenge.

"I don't want to see the film, Mom," I said, edging past her toward the door.

Over the years our dogs had made a path through the woods, and I followed it to a small clearing. Pacing in a tight circle, eyes down and fists clenched, I didn't know what to do. Like so many I would treat later on, I saw no choice but to keep silent, to push it down as far as possible and hope it would all go away. Swilling several stiff drinks after returning to the house, I did my best to act as if nothing had happened, and my mother did the same. We never spoke of it again, and she never attempted another seduction.

While my father had heretofore been the bulwark of traditional norms, in the pre-Zen years of the late 1960s and early 1970s he was experimenting with LSD and growing pot behind his studio. The weighty tone with which he first offered his weed lent an air of formal initiation to the evening, but whether this particular rite confirmed my passage into adulthood, the Matthiessen trinity, or some other transitional dimension was never quite clear. I was always a little guarded on those occasions, not least because getting high with him was never just fun; it was usually freighted with spiritual significance. What was spiritually significant to him, that is. For my part, I had no interest in pursuing satori or nirvana; I just wanted to feel better about myself, something I rarely experienced in his presence.

One evening, sitting in his darkened living room as we passed a joint back and forth, he told Karen and me of how he had seen the face of a rat in the mirror on an acid trip, its nose and whiskers twitching. Deborah walked by as he spoke, silent and ethereal, disappearing into the children's wing to make sure Rue and Alex were asleep. On another occasion, the gloom accentuated by the embers of a dying fire, he gave me a penetrating look before offering to "guide" me on LSD. Trying not to show my ambivalence, I was relieved after several years had passed and he had either forgotten about it or decided I would never be an appropriate candidate.

At lunch one afternoon, he read a letter from Timothy Leary commending him on his description of an acid trip in *At Play in the Fields of the Lord*. When he finished, he noted with a chuckle that the drug in question wasn't LSD, but my interest was piqued and I finally picked up the book. Reading the novel, which I enjoyed far more than I had anticipated, was like looking through a one-way mirror. But while I recognized several of what would become his major themes, it would be another ten years before I appreciated the irony of what had finally drawn me to his work.

When Deborah introduced him to Zen practice, he quickly adopted it as his own. Not long after finishing *At Play*, I went to a Zen temple in New York to try my hand at meditation. This was prompted by my father's amazement at the ease with which I could slap myself into a lotus position, something that was always painfully difficult for him. That I then walked around his living room on my knees, maintaining the lotus the entire time, confirmed me as a natural in his eyes. At eighteen I could see that there was something powerful to be gotten from sitting, if one had the discipline, but I was more interested in sex and getting high.

Later that summer I also began to read Frank's poetry. Since it featured Mike, I started with "Why I Am Not a Painter." Frank came alive on the page, and I could almost hear him reading his lighthearted depiction of how their friendship influenced their work. "To the Harbormaster," a poem of a very different sort, nearly broke my heart. It spoke of longing, a yearning for permanency in love, and the recognition that it can never be had. Like Frank, I was searching for my own harbormaster, already sensing that I might never find him.

Five

WHILE I HADN'T TAKEN PARTICULAR NOTICE OF THEM AT THE time of my interview, Plato, Aristotle, Demosthenes, Cicero, and others, their names engraved in the lintel of Butler Library, seemed to leap out at me as I began my first semester at Columbia. With its ionic pillars and domed ceiling, the building's façade triggered a reflexive tightening in my stomach, somatic evidence of a suspicion that I was in no way prepared for what was about to unfold. Like Chet Pomeroy in Thomas McGuane's *Panama*, I was beginning to sense that "the night had written a check which daylight couldn't cash."

Confronting the rigors of college was like looking down the barrel of a gun, evoking the metabolic and psychological reactions common to a "fight or flight" response. My first class was an overview of the humanities. As if to echo the emanations from the library's lintel, the professor announced that we would start with the *Iliad*. After more preparatory remarks and a review of the general goals of the course, he distributed the syllabus and declared that we were to read the first twelve books of Homer's epic by Wednesday. Since anyone could see that this amounted to a fairly good-sized book in itself, I initially thought he was kidding. When similar expectations were announced in my other classes, it was all I could do not to panic.

By now I was beginning to experience the "son of" phenomenon ("Are you related to Peter Matthiessen?"), and hadn't been entirely surprised when my father was invited to give the commencement address at Solebury. Rather than preparing my own inspirational remarks as class valedictorian, I spent all of graduation eve completing my senior project, without which the school promised to withhold my diploma. Occasionally dozing in the noonday sun, I didn't take in much of his speech.

Along with my father's growing fame, Columbia's heart-stopping syllabi turned an interior spotlight on my boozy indolence. Stoked by fear of failure and increasing doubt about whether I would ever make the grade, my superego went into overdrive, insisting that a fundamental shift in outlook and priorities was called for if I hoped to get by, never mind excel. Before the sun had set on my first week, I was scared straight—at least for a while.

My day was divided between attending classes and completing assignments in a reading room above the sobering lintel. For the first time in several years I knuckled down to study, almost having to reacquaint myself with that skill. I listened carefully to my professors, honing the ability to take succinct but thorough notes. In the quiet of the library I trained myself to read like a student, searching out important themes and ideas. Pen poised, I underlined key passages, seeking a deeper understanding of Achilles's struggle with destiny or the role of the chorus in Greek drama. By exploring the intricacies of Kant and Hegel, I was deliberately going about the business of learning—probing, interpreting, looking for connecting threads, questioning and opening myself to new ideas.

Like St. Paul's, Columbia was still a men's college when I arrived in 1971. To ensure that we received the foundation of a gentleman's education before embarking on a major, all undergrads were required to complete two years of courses in the classics, history, science, philosophy, and a second language. Because it was the logical first step toward becoming a writer, I had already decided to major in English, certain that delving into literature would bring me equal measures of edification, inspiration, and pleasure. In the meantime, I was determined to work hard and steer clear of alcohol.

I missed Karen terribly and saw her as often as possible, but after three months began to worry that our relationship wouldn't survive protracted separations. Burying myself in the library diverted my thoughts for a few hours, but free time was almost intolerable. Willpower finally collapsed on a lonely Saturday night. Crossing Broadway to the Ta-K-Ome deli, I permitted myself a half-gallon jug of "Canadian Ace" beer, which brought on the desired oblivion for less than three dollars. Relieved that I was able to maintain a pattern of weekly drinking while in school, it would be many years before I understood that those who didn't have a problem didn't need to think about controlling it.

Except for the reading room, I never felt at ease in Morningside Heights. Broadway was too wide, the wind from the river too harsh, the feel of the whole too faceless. Nothing seemed to fit comfortably—the university in its urban setting, the more traditional architecture overshadowed by the newer utilitarian brick monoliths, the giant Grecian urns at each end of the main gate across from the Chock Full O' Nuts coffee shop, or the various confirmations of Ivy League legitimacy juxtaposed against the rantings of the schizophrenic homeless man in the 116th St. subway station.

My father and I didn't speak often, but one day he called to say that Deborah had been diagnosed with cancer. The disease spread rapidly throughout her body, and, by the time I got to the hospital, she was past recognizing anyone. Holding her emaciated arms above her head as if grasping for relief, she emitted small gasps of pain with each breath. Several Japanese monks in brown and green silk robes stood by her bed and chanted in bass monotones over the beeping of hospital monitors. The aroma of incense struggled for parity with the pervasive odors of disinfectant and the sweetly acrid smell of dying. I stood in the doorway, held there by an awkward uncertainty as much as a lack of room. My father sat in a chair across from the bed, silently holding his head in both hands. Their marriage had rarely been a happy one, and I didn't envy him his thoughts. Deborah never stopped moaning, and I was struck by how little I knew her. Like her two children, Rue and Alex, she was still a relative stranger, more like a member of someone else's family than the woman who had been my stepmother for nearly ten years.

It was raining when I left the hospital and headed back uptown. My father had thanked me for coming, but I doubted my visit had provided any real solace. Deborah died a few days later, and I drove him home to Sagaponack that night. Barely able to see the road, I had no idea how fast I was going until he said softly, "Slow down, Luke, or you'll kill us, too."

At Christmas I visited Karen and immediately sensed that she was involved with someone else. We took a walk in the cold and quickly fading light, our breath showing white in the still air. A cornfield lay on our right, its harvested stubble rigid in the frozen earth, and a steep hill fell away on our left. Arriving at a small clearing where we had made love many times, she confessed to being in a relationship with an English teacher at Solebury. My heart began to race, and I couldn't speak. Devastated, I didn't know how I would survive this terrible hurt. Neither of us said a word as we walked in near darkness back to her house. Our footsteps echoed in the silence, and woodsmoke was on the wind.

We made love that night, both of us guarded and confused. The sex was almost desperate, meant to push away the finality that was certain to follow. After holding her for what I believed would be the last time, I could see nothing on my horizon but emptiness and despair. Dressing quickly, as if to protect myself, I caught the first train in the morning.

Several weeks later I was still too heartsick to feel much joy upon learning I had made the dean's list. I began to take long walks, the icy river wind blowing tiny tornados of garbage and grit along the pavement. Between classes I often wandered the hilly trails of Morningside Park, stopping to gaze at scudding clouds or the wintery expanse of the Hudson. Night fell by late afternoon, and the side streets were hard to navigate. In the darker patches I occasionally had difficulty seeing the outlines of trash cans or tree guards, sometimes tripping over them, so I kept to the bright lights of Broadway whenever possible.

On weekends I sometimes joined my mother for a wary dinner at her new apartment on Commerce Street, next to a townhouse once owned by Washington Irving. While walking through my old neighborhood provided the comfort of familiarity, my connection to it was increasingly tenuous, like the fraying rope which held his clam basket to my father's waist. The absence of a real home exacerbated a persistent sense of aimlessness, and I longed for a permanent refuge.

The only time I shook off my despondency was when I rendez-voused with Jackie at the White Horse tavern. Drinking with him just a block from where we had grown up was as close as I would ever get to the old days, but for those few hours I could think of nothing better. Cigarette smoke hung over us like a warm blanket, blend-ing with the soothing aroma of stale beer to form an impenetrable barrier against the outside world. The drinks worked their magic to the accompaniment of music and laughter, and I delighted in hearing of how Jackie's mother had taken in Brendan Behan after a hard night at this very bar. Dylan Thomas had downed his last shots of whiskey here, but I preferred to imagine the Irish author asleep on the Hanley's sofa, his host unaware of his identity until the following day. After Jackie walked me to the subway, I always felt like I had let go of a lifeline.

I never stopped thinking about Karen, the passing of time doing little to ease my misery. My grades started to suffer, and I was losing interest in almost everything. "Hey, watch it," a man said, his tone more startled than aggressive. It was an early spring night on Broadway, the sidewalk crowded with students, and I had just collided with him.

"I'm sorry," I replied. "I wasn't looking." Swallowing hard as I readjusted my books, I told myself I must have been preoccupied, lost in thought. Although I couldn't wish away the reality of my decreasing vision, I still didn't believe it was anything serious. Like the memory of my mother's incestuous fantasies, maybe I was hoping the problem would go away if I ignored the symptoms long enough.

Later that spring the campus erupted in demonstrations against the Vietnam War. After the 1968 protests, Columbia was already known as one of the more left-leaning American universities, and the school was once again in the radical vanguard. My spirits revived and I became an unofficial representative of the freshman protestors, a red ribbon tied around my left arm. We had several clashes with the police before I joined a group occupying Kent Hall. For the next two days I slept on the floor, occasionally spoke with journalists, and waited for the cops to storm the building. They finally came in through a basement tunnel, and we beat a hasty retreat through the only unbarricaded window. It would be many years before I recognized the privilege of my position. While I found ways around the draft, young men of lesser means were sent overseas to risk their lives in my place. Without realizing it at the time, I was beginning to confront the inherent contradictions of my politics. Like my parents, I was outspoken and eager to work for social change, but would I ever be willing to forsake the comforts of my surroundings? As unsophisticated and even naive as my efforts were, my youthful zeal kept me from seeing that I already shared their dilemma. For all my radical convictions, I would eventually settle, like them, under the comfortable cloak of the "liberal."

The uprising provided a welcome distraction, even if only for a few days. After we abandoned the buildings and the furor died down, I fell back into the same lugubrious state, uninterested and generally uninspired. Curiosity had given way to indifference, and I knew my name wouldn't reappear on the dean's list. While F. O. had found his niche at Harvard, I was anything but content at Columbia. Lonely and fundamentally disconnected from college life, I began to wonder whether I was really destined to complete the great Matthiessen triad.

Jackie invited me for dinner in early May, and I accepted at once, glad for a break. He had only recently acknowledged that Mel, a computer technician and sailor with thinning hair and horn-rimmed glasses, was his roommate and lover, not an upstairs neighbor who just happened to be around all the time. Relieved that I no longer had to play into that fiction, I was looking forward to their company.

Before joining them I met Mike at the Guggenheim, which was showing a Mondrian retrospective. As we descended the ramp Mike explained how the modernist's geometric abstractions had influenced his own work, his observations as fascinating as the paintings themselves. After parting I decided to ride the Fifth Avenue bus down to the Village. Once past the Central Park Zoo, the bus lurched forward at half-block intervals, hemmed in by midtown traffic. The sidewalks were filled with people shopping at the fancier department stores, and tourists mobbed Rockefeller Center.

Crossing 45th Street, I saw that the corner was "lit up like Luna Park," as Jackie might have said of a drunken acquaintance. Rows of fluorescents shone through the plate glass on the ground floor, topped by Qantas in electric red across the exterior span of the office. The bus slowed to a halt again, and I scanned a map of the seven continents in the window. Set in a large boxed frame, it depicted the airline's numerous routes shooting forth from Australia in spider web filaments. Like the sign above the entrance, the continents were bright red against the blue backdrop of the seven seas.

In studying the map I could see that Australia was about as far away as I could get, and suddenly that was exactly where I wanted to be. Remembering that a cousin had worked on a sheep station in the western part of the country, it occurred to me that I might do the same. At that moment I wanted nothing more than to get away from school, Karen, the question of my future, all of it. Traveling halfway around the world would give me a chance to clear my head and renew my sense of direction, and then there was the promise of adventure. I could sell my car, take a leave of absence and, yes, it could be done. By the time the bus reached the Village I had made up my mind to go.

Jackie and Mel's apartment on Charles Street was a tiny studio, made habitable and even cozy by a seaman's space-saving instincts. Wine glasses hung from a book shelf, the range sat atop a small yellow refrigerator, and the wall clock read "It's time for A & P coffee." I could barely wait to tell them about my plan, and we batted the idea around while Jackie and I played a few rounds of casino. Mel prepared a fine dinner of pork chops, roasted potatoes, and sauerkraut, their rich aromas complemented by the spiced apples we had for dessert.

After dinner we consulted their globe, and I realized that Australia was an ideal place from which to launch a trip around the world. From Singapore I could travel through Southeast Asia, heading west through India, Afghanistan, on to Turkey, through Europe and home. It was an ambitious itinerary, one which would never get off the ground unless I secured both a job and some initial capital beforehand.

Mel thought it might not be wise to leave school for a full year, perhaps fearing that I might never return, and Jackie wondered whether my family would ever endorse anything so extreme. I suggested that the trip might be just the thing to ignite a literary spark, a prospect I was fairly sure would excite my father, and reminded them that travel was an essential component of his work. The more we talked it through, the more determined I became.

After washing up, Jackie declared that it was time to go out and celebrate, but Mel declined to join us. He wasn't a heavy drinker, and probably didn't want to know where Jackie went after I headed uptown. We went barhopping until the wee hours, my expectations for the trip rising with every beer. By the end of the night I was certain my great notion would result in great things. I would come home a world traveler, a young man whose character had been tempered by challenge and adversity. What I was soon to experience would surely inspire a flood of words onto paper, and I would return like the prodigal son, standing proud at the threshold of my destiny. Before we parted Jackie taught me the words to "Waltzing Matilda," and we sang it with tuneless passion as we swayed arm in arm to the subway.

The next day, nearly four years after he had delivered his proclamation, I called my father and presented my plan to work abroad and travel the world. I still hadn't written anything, but hoped that leaving home for so long would cast me, at least superficially, as a "chip off the old block" and garner his favor. He supported the idea wholeheartedly, and I knew my desire to set out on my own had raised me in his estimation.

He ended the conversation by saying that he would write to Ron and Valerie Taylor, the underwater filmmakers, to advise that I would be contacting them in the next few months. Along with my father, they had been on Peter Gimbel's expedition to film the great white shark, an adventure chronicled in Gimbel's film,

Blue Water, White Death, and my father's book, *Blue Meridian*. My fascination with sharks had superseded a lingering reluctance to read his work, and I finished the book in two sittings shortly after its publication. That I might now have the good fortune to work with two of the world's most acclaimed divers was nothing short of thrilling.

Because of my aunt's connection I soon had a letter guaranteeing employment and secured a one-year work visa. After the student protests, it wasn't surprising that Columbia raised no objection to my taking a leave of absence, and Mike offered to sell my car. With the prospective sale as collateral, I was able to borrow the money for airfare and some initial backup. My mother and sister weren't especially happy to see me go, but understood how important this odyssey was to me, the proverbial young man in search of self. Within six weeks of passing the map, both accompanied me to the airport.

Six

AFTER A GRUELING SEQUENCE OF FLIGHTS AND LAYOVERS, I landed at Esperance, a small town on the southwestern coast. Richard Verco, the manager of the Yerritup Creek Station and my new boss, was there to greet me. Short and affable, he had a barrel chest, a strong handshake, and dark, laughing eyes. The Australian winter was coming on, and he was dressed in a thick sweater against the chill which blew across the grass landing strip. I was clad in jeans, a brown leather jacket, a black cowboy hat, and construction boots. I can only imagine what his first impressions were, but he was gracious enough not to share them.

Once we cleared town, which was comprised mainly of car dealerships, farm supply outlets, and hotels featuring both saloon and lounge bars, we drove for seventy-five miles before coming to the station. The ground was generally flat and devoid of trees, and we passed no houses or hamlets. Unbroken stretches of scrub were occasionally punctuated by large tracts of cleared land. So different from anything I had ever seen, this world struck me at first as uniformly dull, barren, monotonous. But it was vast, seemingly endless, and, I would soon appreciate, mysteriously compelling under an eternal sky. When we turned on to a dirt road for the last

71

leg of the journey, I had the sensation of being not just far away, but almost unreachable.

More than our conversation, I recall the intervals of quiet. A gray sky hung motionless as we sped through the bush, the tires raising clouds of dust. I stared straight ahead through rose-tinted aviator glasses, unaware of metaphorical irony. Fingering the cowboy hat on my lap, already wishing I hadn't brought it, I wondered what lay in store.

Forty years later I can still picture myself on that ride, a portrait of that confused stage between adolescence and adulthood, doing my best to appear confident and relaxed. I had taken off with characteristic impetuosity, having only the vaguest notion of what I was seeking. While I hoped to return a grown man, I couldn't have said what that might look like. When Richard announced that we had reached our destination, I was determined to earn my keep, broaden my horizons, and make my father proud.

I had arrived on a Saturday afternoon and was shown my quarters. Along with five others, I was to be a "jackeroo," or ranch hand, and would occupy the one empty cubicle in the unadorned building. Left to myself, I made my bed and prepared to take a nap, since I had been up for nearly two days and the thin mattress on its sparse metal frame looked like it could envelop me in sleep within seconds.

Only the far-off bleating of sheep and a winter wind whistling through wire fence broke the quiet as I began to drift off.

Two cars pulled up and three other jackeroos entered the quarters.

"Goodday, mate," the first said. "I'm Dave, David Jenkins. You must be the new Yank." With shoulder-length dark hair, Dave's rugged features foreshadowed how he would probably look in another thirty years.

"I'm Sadie," another said, extending his calloused hand. "Adrian, really, Adrian Seaford. But everyone calls me Sadie.

Listen, we're just knocking off. We'll wash up, and how about heading into town for a piss-up?" Registering my blank stare, he added, "A night at the bar. It's what we do every Saturday." Like Dave, Sadie was well built but slightly shorter and topped with long blonde hair.

I was exhausted but didn't wish to appear antisocial, so agreed to go.

Over the course of getting acquainted we polished off a pitcher of beer and ordered a second. While awaiting the refill I began playing with my empty glass, absentmindedly turning it over on the table. Sadie grabbed the glass and set it upright. "Listen, mate," he said, "you turn your glass over means you'll fight any cunt in the bar." Since I was a scrawny New Yorker among dozens of brawny Outback types, I never made that mistake again.

When I subsequently heard such remarks as "I ain't got no time for the bloody Abos, mate. Bloody useless race," I began to appreciate that rural Australia in the early seventies, before the country's emergence on the world's cultural stage, was something of an anachronism. My companions were largely ignorant, racist, and not overly curious, but I would learn that they were also some of the funniest, most generous, loyal, and trustworthy people I'd ever met. Once assured that I only sought to be on an equal footing and intended to work hard, we established friendships which, while they never rose to the full status of "mate," were no less important to me.

In addition to four Australians and myself, the remaining jackeroo was an Englishman named Nicholas Braithwaite. The Australians often referred to the English as "Pommies," a term derived from POME (Prisoner of Mother England), which was stamped on the shirts of convicts transported to the horrific penal colonies of the eighteenth and nineteenth centuries. There was generally little love lost between the Aussies and Brits, and Nicky, who looked like an English aristocrat, had a hard time of it at the outset. He was greeted with "Hello, Breastfed" more than once, only half in jest. But as he was good-natured and a capable worker, he, too, was soon accepted into the fold.

Spread out over 150,000 acres, Yerritup Creek Station was home to 75,000 sheep and 500 head of cattle. Along with the six jackeroos and station manager, there were two supervisors, a mechanic and, fifteen miles up the road, a middle-aged American who had emigrated from the Midwest with his wife and two children.

Our work varied considerably but was always dictated by the season or what would yield the most wool. We prepared fields for planting, mended fence, bagged grain, and drove sheep in to be inoculated, drenched, shorn, and branded before driving them back to their paddocks. We butchered sheep, kept the buildings in good repair, and castrated newborn lambs, the older hands using their few remaining teeth.

I loved the hard physical labor. Not just good exercise, there was something meditative about the work, a pleasure in being distracted from thought and subsumed by the natural order of the land. Whether it was clearing a field of roots, feeding a combine with heavy sacks of seed and fertilizer as it bumped along, stacking bales of hay in sweltering heat, or moving thousands of sheep on horseback under the great sky, the day usually ended with a sense of accomplishment no less gratifying than making the dean's list. More than meditation, our work had a way of locking me in the present moment, quieting my ego and its self-centered worries— would I ever measure up? What would happiness look like, if it could be had at all? Hard work tended to block out past guilt and the anxiety I always felt when contemplating my future. "Be here now," I'd read again and again, but had never before pulled it off. At times I wondered whether my father had experienced something similar during his days as a haul seiner, but never remembered to ask.

As I scanned the horizon at first light, I always felt a sense of renewal, a connection to something timeless, so it was only natural that my favorite chore was milking the cows. Rising before dawn, I drove one of the trucks to the milking shed, where two cows waited by the gate. Once the engine was shut off, the only sounds in the awakening gray were the swishing of tails and the stirrings of unseen birds. The smells of hay and manure suffused the air, and the creaking of the gate was so loud in the stillness that I thought I might wake those sleeping nearby.

My charges took their places at once, dipping their heads into the trough as I readied them for milking. To my delight, I discovered they always gave more when I played classical music on the radio. Resting my head against their huge flanks while I listened to Shubert and seduced streams of milk from their udders never felt like work.

By sunrise I had a full bucket, still warm in the morning chill, attuned to the world in ways I had never been before. Then came the challenge of balancing the milk outside the truck with one hand while steering with the other, not an easy feat on pitted roads and having to work a gearshift. Despite such a severe test of my motor skills, I usually managed to deliver the milk to the various quarters without spilling too much.

Planting began in earnest about two months after my arrival. The station had two tractors, and one afternoon I accidentally steered the largest into a support pole of the main shed, leaving a sharply angled dent. To make matters worse, the incident was witnessed by the mechanic and two jacks, and all three applauded as I climbed down to inspect the damage. Richard wasn't pleased, but the pole didn't require repair and stood as a humiliating reminder of my inexperience.

The fields were plowed before the soil was further readied by the processes of scarifying and harrowing, the last stage rendering the dirt into soft, malleable rows. Because it was essential that the crop reach full maturity before harvest, all hands felt the pressure to complete the spring planting on time, and one tractor was always manned well into the night.

I was on edge when it was my turn for night duty. The task itself wasn't so difficult, nothing more than making contiguous rows with the scarifier. I had done it during daylight hours and tried to reassure myself that I wouldn't have any trouble.

Everything went smoothly until I completed my first pass and turned the tractor around. No matter how I strained, I couldn't see the rows I had just made. Sitting alone on that cold night, the tractor's engine idling loudly, I hadn't been so close to tears since breaking down when telling my father of how miserable I was at St. Paul's. What could I say to the others? Why should they believe that I couldn't see? Desperate, I kept going, the tractor's headlights of no use except to alert me to an approaching fence. Hoping the rows I was making were at least close to where they should've been, I continued for another half-hour before returning the tractor to the shed, sickened by the thought of what would be revealed in the morning.

Apart from milking, our day typically began at eight, when we gassed up the vehicles and were assigned our tasks. Richard sent everyone else off before asking me to stay with him, and we drove to the top of a rise which overlooked the field I had worked the night before. Rather than acres of parallel lines, what lay before us was a mess of uneven rows, many crossing others at strange angles.

Looking over the chaos, Richard asked what had happened. After a pause I apologized and explained that I hadn't been able to see in the dark. I had tried but just couldn't see the rows to guide me. Richard didn't respond for several moments. He didn't seem angry so much as bewildered, at a loss. At last he asked whether I had known about this problem before coming to the station. I admitted that I had occasionally experienced some difficulty seeing at night, but never thought it would be this bad and hadn't tried to hide anything. In the silence which followed I think we both understood that this wasn't entirely true, but Richard had no way of knowing that, more than lying about my history, I was in denial of it.

Because I couldn't work at night, it was decided that I would be the only one to take tractor duty on Sundays. The other jacks readily accepted this, since they could sleep in after a long week and a night in town. To my great relief, everyone was supportive and did what they could to help.

As Sadie had explained on my first day, we went into Esperance every Saturday night. It was the only time most of us left the station, and I began to look forward to that weekly respite like someone else might anticipate a special holiday. We all needed a break, but I don't believe anyone looked forward to drinking like I did. I always got drunk, and sometimes didn't remember the ride back. One night, for a change of pace, we went to a drive-in. The feature was *Lawrence of Arabia*, and the others loaded up on beer at the concession stand. Not sure I could find the men's room in the dark, I bought a bottle of Cointreau, which prompted some good-natured ribbing. Just after the great scene where the sun rises slowly over the desert, I blacked out.

The diesel engine was deafening in the early morning quiet, much louder than I remembered, and my head was splitting. Towing the harrows over the large field, I wasn't sure which was worse, the relentless jostling or the toxic fumes, and I regretted the previous night's excesses yet again. It was my third Sunday on the tractor, and the morning seemed to drag on forever. At last I finished and stopped to inspect my work. From one end to the other, the rows were perfect.

Several weeks later, when scores of acres blossomed into beautiful green lines, I had never felt so fulfilled. "I did that. I really did that," I thought as I looked out across the field. It was an extraordinary sensation, and I took proprietary umbrage when kangaroos dared to violate the wonder of my achievement.

"Something's wrong," Dave said one afternoon as we passed the small paddock near the milking shed. "She's not right." He stopped the truck and we climbed over the fence. A brown and white heifer, accidentally impregnated when too young and small, was in distress while calving. Lying on her side, she was breathing heavily, her eyes wild. "That damned bull," Dave muttered. "I hope we can save her."

Over the next hour we took turns trying to pull out the calf, bracing our feet against her hindquarters. At last it emerged, stillborn, and the three of us lay exhausted. Ten minutes later the heifer finally raised her head to sniff her calf, nudging it gently. Stroking her side, neither of us spoke as flies began to settle on the small carcass. She rose when Dave placed the calf in the back of the truck, walking beside me as I followed. Had he seen how tightly I held her, eyes turned toward the sky, and my reluctance to leave?

I remained at Yerritup Creek for six months before heading off to join Ron and Valerie Taylor. Over that time I had grown deeply attached to the place, the other men, and especially the work. A few weeks before leaving I began to ride out into the bush on my day off to experience the land in solitude. Sitting atop my horse on those hot summer afternoons, a shirt covering my head against the sun, I tried to meditate on the openness, the dust-covered scrub, the birds, an occasional snake, the warm earth smells, and the ringing echo of the horse's hoof against a rock. Alone in the vastness of the bush, I felt a powerful sense of belonging. I knew I would miss being on the land, but also understood that I couldn't stay.

As we stood before his house, Richard said, "Thanks for all your hard work and dedication, Luke."

"You're welcome, Richard, but I should be doing the thanking. I'll never forget my time here."

Speaking softly, he continued, "You know, in many ways you were the best of the lot."

Not just surprised, I was shocked. I had never excelled at any of the duties we all performed, the others had more experience and two had even grown up on sheep stations. Although I was now in the best shape of my life, they were stronger and generally more capable. "Well, thanks again, but we both know that's not exactly true."

"I'm talking about what you gave to it, how this was more than just a job for you. That's what matters. You did excellent work, and I wish I had five more like you." We shook hands, and I instantly regretted not being able to complete a full year's cycle with him. Before parting I decided that Richard's gift was best kept to myself, and never told my father about that exchange.

The Taylors were shooting a television series entitled *Inner Space*, and I crossed the continent on the back of Nicky's motorcycle to assist in the filming of thirty-minute episodes on nurse and leopard sharks. Looking out across the unbroken expanse of the Nullarbor Plain, road wind and engine noise silencing everything but my thoughts, there was plenty of time to reflect. While I had left home with the idea that I would go on an adventure and become a writer almost as a matter of course, I hadn't packed paper or pen and had no inclination even to keep a journal. Neither had I brought any books, so my reading was largely limited to the English World War II comics favored by the other jacks. Any therapist would have jumped on such a discrepancy, but at the time I attached little significance to it.

Before joining Ron and Valerie I spent two days in Sydney and had prescription lenses fitted to the inside of a face mask, which gave me the appearance of a myopic creature from the greatest depths of the Mariana Trench. When I knocked on the screen door of their suburban home, a female voice sang out a welcome and asked that I bring in the milk. Walking to the back of the house, I found the Taylors looking over some papers at the kitchen table. Valerie was dressed in shorts and a white blouse. An attractive woman, she had high cheekbones, bright eyes, and platinum blonde hair. Ron, who was clad in a black Speedo and blue polo shirt, greeted me in warm undertones as he stood to shake my hand. In their early forties, they looked exactly as they had in *Blue Water, White Death*.

Valerie almost shrieked when I placed the milk on the table, and for an instant I thought I must have done something terribly wrong. She explained that this was the first time it had come in a plastic bottle and rose to make a phone call. Within hours of the milk's arrival she was on television, educating thousands on how plastic waste was choking the Australian reefs. Although I was determined to be as helpful as possible, it was clear from the start that I would be getting by far the better end of our bargain.

Late that afternoon I went with Valerie to a public pool where she taught me the basics of safe diving—buddy breathing, clearing my mask underwater, and the like. To lessen my fear of being at close and unprotected proximity, we went to the shark tank at the Sydney Aquarium the next day. She instructed me to stand in the corner once we submerged, and to remain motionless while she filmed an enormous grouper who also resided there.

Over the side we went, and I found my corner as Valerie set out after the grouper. The sharks, which had been lazily circling the perimeter, initially reacted to our presence by swimming in quick, erratic bursts. I kept my eye on them at first, but began to watch Valerie photographing the grouper after they started to settle down. Sensing something off to my left, I turned to find a large nurse shark within inches of my face mask, its rapier-like teeth moving almost imperceptibly. Rattled, I decided to keep this one in sight. When it came around again, passing close enough to brush my belly with its pectoral fin, I touched its sandpaper skin. The shark scurried off, afterward remaining at a safer distance.

The next step was a practice dive on a boulder-strewn reef not far from shore. I swam independently, descending below the swells to a depth of about twenty feet. The reef was shaded with muted greens and browns, and the contrast of the brightly colored fish against the undulating plant life was stunning. Mesmerized by the seascape and the sensation of weightlessness, I floated along the rocky bottom as if in orbit around an alien world.

Something tugged at my air gauge, which I had ignored since getting into the water. After I met her stern gaze, Valerie pointed its face toward me. It read empty, and she jabbed at the surface. Startled and embarrassed, I had learned my lesson. On the drive back to Sydney I replayed the dive and realized that I hadn't seen Valerie approaching. As much as I would have preferred to think otherwise, I knew this wasn't entirely because I had been oblivious to everything but the splendors of the deep.

After working our way up the coast of New South Wales, stopping twice to take footage of nurse sharks, we arrived just over the border of Queensland in search of the leopard shark. Although large, this species is harmless, relying on crushing plates instead of teeth to feed on mollusks and crustaceans. It was known to frequent several reefs in the region, and its spots were sure to make for unusual footage.

We had two days of excellent filming, marred only by the arrival of a whaler shark. About ten feet long, it came in from deeper water, its menacing gray looking almost out of place among the brightly colored coral. Swimming easily, with no apparent aggression, the whaler approached Valerie twice, each time receiving a bump on the snout from the housing of her still camera. Because it ignored three other divers before heading off, Ron later theorized that the shark had been lured by her blonde hair. Typical of her, Valerie minimized any danger, probably hoping to allay the anxiety the rest of us felt.

After a heavy rain the sea was muddied by drainage from a

nearby river, so there was no hope of filming. Ron and I played chess and ate a bucket of prawns to pass the time. Usually more reticent than his wife, he delighted me with his deadpan delivery of several amusing but fondly recalled anecdotes about my father, all of which have now slipped from memory. When the game was over, I filled the tanks and checked that everything was ready for the next day's filming before going out for a walk.

Passing a pub, I stopped to weigh the consequences. I hadn't thought about drinking since joining the Taylors but, as I stared inside, the urge was powerful. Because I had never seen them have so much as a glass of wine, I wasn't sure how they would react to my imbibing on my own. Also concerned about word getting back to my father, I didn't relish the possibility of being reprimanded for having embarrassed him. Finally deciding to ignore the risk, I passed through the open door and had two pints. If Ron and Valerie suspected my waywardness on that occasion, they never mentioned it, and I finished my time with them in good standing.

In a letter she sent my father after my departure, Valerie wrote, "Luke has left us and we all miss him. He could've stayed with us forever." She continued, "Luke is one of those people who naturally attracts danger. The fish he wanted to spear had deadly poisonous flesh, and the shell he found and carried around was the biggest venomous cone I have ever seen. There were dozens of shells and he chose that one. But most of all, he seems to have no fear of anything, and this worried Ron and myself the most." She concluded: "Send him back any time. We will take him in a shot."

My separation from the Taylors was precipitated, in part, by the approach of a major cyclone to the northeastern coast. Ron and Valerie decided to head south, reversing the northward track we had taken from Sydney. Because I had now been in Australia for eight months, I chose to continue in the other direction, through the Northern Territories and on to Asia. As hard as it was to leave them, it was time to move on. Placing the carefully wrapped venomous cone in the bottom of my backpack, I would present it to my grandmother, still smelling, shortly after my return.

Over the next five months I traveled from Singapore to Istanbul, a journey of contrasts as much as discovery. While Bangkok appeared to be another casualty of the Vietnam war, with legions of young prostitutes catering to whatever "Joe" or "Billy" might want on R & R, a white-haired woman dressed all in black offered her blessing by pouring a trickle of water over my head during the annual Song Kran festival in Chiang Mai. After I reciprocated, we smiled, bowed to one another, and went our separate ways.

I was horrified by the ravages of Calcutta. With more than a million people living on its streets, I had no previous conception of poverty on this scale, or that the daily routine of any metropolis might include the collection of the dead from sidewalks and alleyways. Deliberately maimed children in rags swarmed around me, their cupped hands and desperate eyes pleading for small change or a scrap of food. "*Baksheesh, sahib, baksheesh,*" they droned, prompting simultaneous feelings of pity, helplessness, and a desire to flee.

Apart from accentuating my white skin and privilege, pointing an expensive camera at so much despair seemed almost predatory, an arrogant assertion of my own comfort and security, and I decided to put it away, next to the venomous cone. I never regretted that decision and have no doubt that it helped me pay more attention to the places I visited. Rather than chronicling my experiences, I wanted to live them, as contrary to good journalistic practice as that surely was. Rising at dawn five days later, I could just make out the peak of Everest, three hundred miles distant, from a hilltop in Darjeeling.

In Nepal I rowed out to a tiny island in a mountain lake. At its center was a simple Buddhist shrine, with two small bowls in front of the statue. Above me and reflected in the lake towered Annapurna, and the air was silent. Years later, when we compared impressions of our travels through this region, my father recalled thinking, "If I can't get a book out of this, I should be taken out and shot." Sitting alone on that island as I looked up at the snow-covered peaks, it was impossible to ignore the transcendent power of the place, or the breathtaking presence of a roughly crafted metal bowl under the light of heaven.

Under the midday sun of Agra, in quite a different state of transport, I burst into tears at first sight of the Taj Mahal. A monument to one of history's fabled loves, its beauty registered on a visceral level. Later that day I reasoned that drinking three or four bottles of delicious Indian beer before passing through its gate had infused my mood with maudlin sentimentality, but no amount of rationalization can permanently silence a wounded heart.

Today I wonder whether, in contemplating the Taj's perfection, the alcohol hadn't sparked a second acknowledgment of grief. Could this have been the first time I felt genuine sadness, however indirect, at the prospect of losing my vision? Contemplating my future, like reliving that last night with Karen, was simply too painful, a reality I had gone halfway around the world to escape. That day I was frightened of what alcohol had unleashed, so much so that I was relieved to learn I would have no access to booze while traveling through several Muslim countries to the west.

I didn't know it then, but the emergence of grief would spark the beginnings of spiritual growth, a process which was never linear and inevitably followed undeniable loss. What I feared was precisely where the work of healing would begin. When I eventually allowed myself to "look" at my impending blindness, stared into it, I was a little less threatened, a little less afraid.

Before crossing the Khyber Pass into Afghanistan, I recoiled at the sudden appearance of a Pakistani leper pressed against the bus's window, his features half eaten away. In less than a week I would be transfixed by two standing Buddhas, both carved out of a mountainside in Bamiyan. The statues were monumental, one rising to a height of 165 feet. Looking up at them was like following the trajectory of a cathedral's spire into the firmament. Mohammed's armies had removed their faces twelve hundred years earlier, rendering their presence all the more mysterious and compelling. Would I ever experience anything approaching their quiet tranquility, their victory over blindness? After nightfall I stayed close to my room. Like the Buddhas, I no longer saw well enough to navigate the village's dimly lighted streets. But I can still picture them today, their inspirational power enduring despite being destroyed by the Taliban in 2001.

The mountains of Band-e-Amir were rounded as if by centuries of erosion, the accumulated dust of countless millennia covering them almost to their summits. Turbaned men on spirited ponies rode by, as proud as their horses. In the warm spring breeze, occasionally chilled by strong gusts from the higher peaks to the east, I was awed by the barren beauty of the place, the blue diamond brilliance of the region's lakes amid what seemed to be the world's oldest landscape. That day I wanted nothing more than to don the turban I had purchased in Kabul and ride one of the ponies deeper into the mountains, where I might merge forever with the land and its people, far away from accountability, loneliness, and the expectations of others.

I had heard nothing but dire warnings about the Turks from almost every traveler I met on the way west, so was on high alert when I finally entered the country. As I strolled the streets of a Black Sea port, worried that I might not have enough money to get home, a middle-aged man took my arm and beckoned me toward an alley. I decided to follow, resigning myself to whatever fate was in store.

But instead of finishing me off, the man brought me to a restaurant and motioned to a chair. He spoke in animated Turkish, accompanying his words with elaborate bows and hand gestures. I told him that I didn't understand, and a plate of black olives and goat cheese was placed on the table. This was soon followed by an enormous platter of grilled fish, rice, and vegetables. When I pulled out my pockets to indicate that I had no money, he seemed only to take offense and encouraged me to eat. Famished, I obeyed while he stood over me and smiled, still not convinced this wouldn't be my last supper.

After stuffing myself on the best meal I'd had in months, I again protested that I couldn't pay. My host, apparently the restaurant's owner, indicated that I should remain seated until he returned. Coffee was brought while I waited, and he came back with another man who, in broken English, asked me to write down my name and address. When I handed the owner the slip of paper, he smiled and said, "My American friend."

I arrived in Victoria Station a week later, having taken the Orient Express from Istanbul. Standing before a mirror for the first time in four months, I couldn't suppress a small gasp. My face was gaunt, with hollow cheeks and sunken eyes, my body almost skeletal. After purchasing a charter plane ticket I had only forty dollars for a week in London, and that wouldn't cover my shared room. I had accumulated a number of semiprecious stones and various artifacts which I planned to give to family and friends, but now began hawking these in front of a hotel frequented by American tourists. Doubtlessly looking a bit strange in my sandals and green pajama suit, I probably sounded exactly like the merchants I had bargained with all the way across Asia. Nevertheless, I managed to get enough money to see me through the week, and filled myself with as much rich food and stout as I could hold.

My backpack was the first piece of luggage off the plane, and I girded myself for what I was certain would be a tough time at customs. But despite having visited some of the world's most notorious drug-producing countries and probably looking like a junkie, I was ushered through without so much as a second glance. My mother and sister were waiting on the other side of the door, and I was overjoyed to see them.

"Ulie!" Carey shouted, and ran to hug me. A reversal of Lee Krasner's "Lulu," the nickname had stuck. At eighteen she had left her girlish looks behind and was now a beautiful young woman, with a stylish haircut and the subtlest hint of makeup. In that moment I felt a surge of love for her, like when we were little and each other's favorite companion. Adolescence and living apart had put some distance between us, but I had never been happier to see anyone.

My mother approached, smiling as she began to weep. She looked shorter, slightly hunched in a skirt and khaki jacket. We embraced, and I held her without reservation. I would never forget that exchange in the hallway, but it felt safe to love her again. Frightened by how thin I was, she didn't let go of my arm until we reached the car.

I had been away for thirteen months and was now twenty years a' growing. The trip had matured me, transforming my perspective on life in ways I hadn't yet defined. I had experienced wonderful things, overcoming fear and uncertainty along the way, and done it on my own. Now a world traveler in my own right, I had stretched the $700 I had saved from my $35-a-week salary at Yerritup Creek over three continents. No longer so idealistic or naive, my travels had seasoned me, broadening my interests and capabilities, if not confirming exactly what direction these might take. As proud as I was fatigued, I had done it.

On the way out to Springs, at his request, we stopped at my father's house. My mother and sister waited in the car while I went inside, where not even his dog stirred. The large living room was lighted by two Japanese lamps mounted on the wall, and his bedroom door was closed.

I stood still for a moment, listening for any sound, before knocking softly. After a minute the door opened and my father appeared.

Smiling broadly, I awaited a hero's welcome, the paternal equiv-
alent of a ticker tape parade, the accolades he'd been aching to
shower on his prodigal son.

"It's good to see you, Luke," he whispered, and asked if I would
call in the morning. Many years went by before I could acknowledge that my expectations had been somewhat unreasonable, especially given the late hour. Now I can't remember when I called,
but it wasn't the next day.

Carey screamed when I came into the kitchen. I had taken off
my shirt and was hoping to find something to eat. She stood up,
backing away, and said she could see my heart beating. I thought
she might be exaggerating until I recalled how disturbed I had
been at first sight of my emaciated body. Subsequent tests revealed
that I was hosting stomach parasites, probably picked up in northern Thailand, but the medication I was given quickly reversed the
problem.

Since I hadn't disappeared into the Australian bush or the
mountains of Afghanistan, I needed to plot a course. I hadn't ruled
out becoming a writer but was beginning to consider editing as
an acceptable alternative. Looking up through the fronds of two
hanging plants as I stretched out on the window seat, I imagined
myself concealed by Malaysian jungle. But as much as I wished
to avoid thinking about my future, I knew I could no longer hide
from the reality of my worsening vision. Talking it over with my
mother as she sunned herself on the beach, I agreed to make an
appointment with Dr. David Pearce, a well-respected ophthalmol-
ogist and family friend.

Short and prematurely bald, David's rounded features matched
his kind and gentle personality. But like a mime waving a hand
over his face to signal a change of emotion, his expression tightened as he ran through his tests. At last he sat back on his stool and
looked directly at me. The corners of his mouth had turned down
and his body appeared to sag, like a balloon the day after a party.

Emphasizing that he wasn't equipped to make a definitive diagnosis, he suggested I contact Dr. Elliot Berson at the Massachusetts Eye and Ear Infirmary.

The next day Carey declared that we needed to have some fun. She was soon to begin her first year at Bennington College, so it would be a while before we got another chance. Like many New Yorkers, we had never been to the top of the Empire State Building, and set off for 34th Street in high spirits. After completing a turn around the observation deck, we couldn't resist getting our portrait taken with King Kong. It had been many years since we'd had such a great time, and it felt good to rekindle a spirit of play. Along with the photograph of my cat sitting on Bill de Kooning's chest, the picture would remain a fixture on our mother's desk for the rest of her life.

Seven

ONE OF THE GREAT IRONIES OF ADDICTION IS THAT ENSLAVE-ment is often mistaken for freedom. As if just released from a four-year prison stretch, I started to drink daily after graduating from college. Several weeks later, I began to yearn for those nights when, returning home from work and the liquor store, I could shut out the world. With the first swallows of liquid warmth coursing through me, I felt safe, unassailable, at peace, unaware that I had already crossed the line into chronic alcoholism.

George Plimpton lived above the *Paris Review*'s tiny office at the eastern end of 72nd Street. When in town he always came down to ask about the day's business—whether suitable art had been found for the next issue, whether everything had gone off to the typesetter or, always a top priority, whether we had secured more ads. After Molly McKaughan, the managing editor, left to fill the same position at a new magazine called *Quest*, he occasionally appeared in a tennis shirt and boxer shorts, carrying his enormous cat, Mr. Puss.

Fayette Hickox was promoted to replace Molly, and under his stewardship the office often throbbed to a disco beat. With the volume at club level, Fayette practically danced in his chair as he typed. Sometimes I marveled that the framed covers of the magazine which decorated the walls didn't fall, one by one, as in a movie scene depicting an earthquake. "Burn, baby, burn," the song boomed. "Burn that mother down."

Fayette was a curious amalgam of the traditional and bohemian. He dressed in clothes purchased from Brooks Brothers' boys department, and liked to keep company with Gerard Malanga, Sylvia Miles, and other denizens of Andy Warhol's Factory. On any given day he might have been seen having lunch at the New York Women's Exchange and later at an opening featuring the works of Robert Mapplethorpe. Effectively fusing my parents' two worlds with an ease I had never thought possible, he was equally comfortable with the elder statesmen of the literary world and the latest arrivals on the downtown scene. Funny and charming, he was a loyal friend.

By contrast, I was on edge in social situations, and usually preferred to avoid them. Instead of seeking out all that was unfolding on the New York cultural stage in the late seventies—the Soho art scene, the opening of the Lower East Side music club CBGB—I was withdrawing into myself. At twenty-two, I had started to put up walls, keeping others at bay with sarcasm and irritability, hoping these passed for erudition and wit. Like my vision, my world was shrinking.

When not fulfilling other duties for George or the magazine, I moved to an old armchair in the corner, trailing a brimming wire basket. This contained the "slush pile," a term often applied to unsolicited manuscripts in the publishing field. Grabbing a small stack of rejection slips and, on occasion, a mild tranquilizer, I got to work.

As its name would suggest, the slush pile usually received short and unceremonious shrift. With the office pulsating to Donna Summer or the Pointer Sisters, I apportioned only a few minutes to work on which its author had probably labored for many hours. Those who hadn't been disillusioned after repeated rejection included carefully crafted cover letters and a self-addressed stamped envelope, in which both their manuscript and the anonymous rejection notice could be returned.

Tossing one of these into the "outgoing" mail basket, I always felt the slightest twinge of guilt. While the vast majority didn't merit publication, their authors had made the effort, stuck their necks out, and I'd never had the courage to do the same. Perhaps I feared a similar reception, or maybe I just had nothing to say. In any case, at my core, I always felt like a fraud.

Fayette and I sometimes joined several friends at the Lower Manhattan Ocean Club on Chambers Street. Mickey Ruskin, who had opened the legendary Max's Kansas City, was its proprietor. In exchange for an ad in the magazine we had what was effectively a bottomless tab, since Mickey never seemed to care that we had long since exceeded our original limit. Talking Heads had a standing gig, a lot of coke was inhaled in the basement bathrooms, and everyone had a great time. Before heading back uptown, we often closed out the night at Dave's Corner, where we had one of New York's best egg creams in hopes of staving off the next day's hangover.

But despite such high times on the town, I preferred to drink alone. My liaisons, when they happened, were spontaneous, brief, and without expectation. Karen wrote to declare, if not her undying love, at least a rekindled affection and desire to try again. She was finishing up at Vassar and came down for the weekend. As excited as I was to see her, I drank too much at dinner, and our lovemaking was tentative and mutually disappointing.

The bedroom was bathed in sunlight as we sipped our coffee the next morning. Karen asked me to read a short story about her mother's recent death. "I knew I looked great," she had written in describing her arrival at the funeral. Because I interpreted this as a sign of an inchoate narcissism, the line triggered a profound sense of loss. After finishing the story I drew a deep breath and declared that a reunion wouldn't work, suggesting she return to Poughkeepsie. Later, I couldn't escape the certainty that I'd been more afraid of a second rejection. That night, depressed and alone, I said goodbye to love by drinking as much as I could before losing consciousness.

1977 was also a difficult year for my father, the most trying of his problems dovetailing with my own. Deeply saddened to learn that his mother had been killed in a car accident, he was relieved to have reconciled with her several years earlier. Standing in his kitchen shortly after the memorial, both of us avoiding the pots Maria had hung at head level, he told me that he had declined a chance to buy the Fishers Island house at a fire-sale price. Outwardly supporting his decision, I inwardly mourned the loss of another piece of my past.

Sometime that fall, probably at Thanksgiving, he asked to speak with me after dinner. The evening's fire had almost burned out, the last logs crumbling into ash as we moved to the sofa in the dim light of the Japanese lamps. Prefacing what he had to say by telling me that it would be best if I heard it first from him, in case it ever got out, he revealed that he had been in the CIA while in France. I was shocked but said nothing, sensing his need to continue.

His speech was even and steady, but he kept his eyes down. He had been recruited while still at Yale, his enlistment having no connection to my grandfather Southgate's association with the OSS. Explaining that the Soviet Union looked like a genuine threat so soon after the war, he had felt a certain patriotic calling. It seemed like a harmless way to support his family, and had the added benefit of leaving him plenty of time to write. He paused for a moment, shifting his position, and told me that the *Paris Review* had been started, at least in part, as a plausible cover for him. "The CIA just wasn't as sinister back then as it is now. But when they asked me to spy on some of my friends, I got out quick."

For a moment I didn't know what to say. It was almost impossible to reconcile this news with everything I knew, or thought I knew, about his history and values, the reasons I had always esteemed him. Nevertheless, I didn't think he deserved condemnation. Deep down I felt a fleeting disappointment and a vague sense of betrayal, but could also appreciate his judgment. Would I have made the same decision had I been in his place? I didn't think so, but couldn't be sure. Nevertheless, given how his politics had shifted so dramatically since that time, it was obvious that this information could compromise his reputation and relationships with friends and those he championed.

I thanked him for his candor, but he kept silent, his eyes still averted. Assuring him that I perceived his dilemma, I added that I was glad he had found his way out. "So am I," he replied with a laugh. Patting my knee as he got up, he said he wanted to read before going to bed, and we wished each other a good night. Left to myself, I had several drinks before going upstairs.

George decided to host a party in early December, and Fayette and I were charged with inviting the many literati, entertainers, and New York elite who typically made up the guest list. His apartment overlooked the East River and was decorated with posters created for the magazine by Lichtenstein, Warhol, Rauschenberg, Kelly, Steinberg, and others, the ideal backdrop for a sophisticated uptown revel.

On the night of the party it was difficult to move among the crowd, and just as hard to hear above the din of laughter, shouts, and repartee. Hovering near the bar, I chatted with acquaintances and didn't think to limit my drinking. Just before leaving, almost as if watching someone else, I told a stranger, a man in his late thirties or early forties, about my father's CIA involvement. Then I went home and passed out.

The roar of garbage trucks woke me the next morning, further jangling my already frayed nerves. Although I couldn't recall the man's name or profession, I remembered what I had said well

enough. Sickened, I attempted to convince myself that, in all likelihood, no real harm had been done, and vowed never to be so
irresponsible again.

Maria had begun a tradition of celebrating Christmas and
Hanukkah on Christmas Eve. Everyone's place at table was designated by a party favor and a name card hand-painted by Paul
Davis. Before dinner the candles on the tree were lit, Handel took
his proper place on the turntable, and Maria suggested that Santa
should make his appearance. I went upstairs and, when given the
cue from below, stomped on the floor, shook a set of sleigh bells,
and belted out my best "Ho, ho, ho!" In the deepest baritone I
could muster, I asked Alex, Sarah, and Antonia whether they
had been good and kind to others. When they affirmed their wor-
thiness, I renewed my stomping, sang out a last "Ho, ho, ho," and
wished everyone a happy holiday, my voice gradually fading with
the reindeer sounds. Presents were then discovered in the fire-
engine red barrel Santa had left behind.

Even though she was now too old to suspend disbelief, I could
see that the embers of Rue's Christmas wonder had also been
fanned. Some years earlier Carey had announced her preference
to be addressed by her given name, Sara. To distinguish her from
Sarah Koenig, she was thereafter referred to as "Sara Carey" among
the family. That night she and my father were getting along, discussing her upcoming *Paris Review* interview with John Gardner.
She was lighthearted and funny and seemed happy to be with the
family. Before the end of the meal, we popped our party favors and
donned the paper crowns hidden inside.

I had almost stopped worrying about my indiscretion when,
three days later, the *New York Times* published a story on the
CIA's efforts to establish a worldwide propaganda network. My
father's involvement was listed as an example of how the agency
had employed various authors and publishers to disseminate its
message. Panicked, I didn't know what to do.

I couldn't confide in anyone, far less confess, and knew only one way to cope.

* * *

While I hadn't been consciously angry with my father, my mother maintained an unwavering antipathy toward him until her death, more than forty years after their divorce. Her mouth always tightened at the mention of his name, and she became visibly agitated in his presence. This was never more apparent than at the twenty-fifth anniversary celebration of the *Paris Review*. Held at Elaine's in the spring of 1978, the party was attended by scores of the magazine's friends and supporters, many of them known to both my parents.

Always uncomfortable at gatherings of those more closely aligned with my father, the mainstream literary crowd, she was anxious from the start and drank far too much. Carefully limiting my own drinking on that occasion, I was talking with my father when she approached, unsteady on her feet and with rage in her eyes. Fixing his gaze and pointing a finger at me, she asked, "Why did you have to cut his balls off?" We stood in silence for several seconds, my mother swaying slightly as she held his eye. Perplexed and embarrassed, I said I would get her a cab.

"Do you have any idea what that was about?" my father asked when I returned.

"None at all," I replied, relieved when he let it drop.

The next day, wondering whether she remembered anything, I decided not to ask. Like the disclosure of her incestuous fantasies, I thought it best not to open that door again.

* * *

That summer, without preamble and almost under his breath,

George said, "I wish I could write like your father." By then he had built a remarkable career out of casting himself as an amateur among the pros, publishing several books and contributing regularly to *Sports Illustrated*, but few considered him a serious writer. Sitting in the office of the magazine he had kept alive for a quarter century, I had never seen him look so wistful.

While sympathetic, I didn't respond. I had bailed out of becoming a writer, and the accolades being heaped on my father after the publication of *The Snow Leopard* shone a progressively irritating light on that fact. Add to this the persistent rawness of my breach, and any mention of my father's writerly prowess usually prompted me to change the subject.

I still hadn't addressed the reality of my worsening eyesight in any meaningful way, but Dr. Berson launched a study to determine whether higher doses of vitamin A might arrest the progression of retinitis pigmentosa. "I need some pioneers to go on a journey with me," he said when we met. I readily agreed, and not just because his was the only reasonable treatment at the time. His manner was notably different. Warm and genial, he was grateful for my willingness to participate. He would eventually enlist six hundred "pioneers," placing us on varying doses of vitamin A, vitamin A mixed with vitamin E, vitamin E by itself, or a placebo. Because his was a double-blind study designed to run over three years, neither he nor I would know what I had been taking until its conclusion. Just before leaving I was given two bottles of capsules, unmarked except for a numerical code, and told that refills would be mailed to me.

While my father was reaching what may well have been the pinnacle of his career, I was on quite a different trajectory. Lisa had been a year ahead of me at Solebury, and we reconnected after she moved into the apartment directly below mine. With blonde hair, green eyes, and Irish good looks, she was outgoing and brash, with a "damn the consequences" approach to life. Her father headed up the public relations efforts for the Metropolitan Museum, and she hoped to follow in his footsteps. She had recently ended a relationship with Jed Horne, a *Time-Life* editor and friend of Molly's I would get to know well. Lisa also loved to drink, and we celebrated our shared affinity by moving in together.

A few months later, dead drunk, I got down on one knee. Deliberately slurring my words in what I imagined was a great joke, I took her hand and asked her to marry me. She sobered up at once and gave her consent. Inwardly kicking myself, I could only hope she would forget about it by morning. The next day she wasted no time before testing my sincerity, and I paused to reflect on my response. Reasoning that I was already twenty-five and might never do it otherwise, I reiterated my proposal. That a more rational voice lurked somewhere within was evidenced when, at the ceremony, my knees shook so badly that my father kept one leg out in the aisle, ready to catch me.

Despite her improprieties, I loved my mother as much as ever, and she was great fun to be around. She had built a second house in Springs shortly after the first burned down, and we visited often. Joe LeSueur, also a frequent guest, dubbed it "Casa Neurotica." The house was usually crowded with friends, music played loudly, and good times were generally had by all. Sara Carey, who was now seeing Jed, was put off by everyone's drinking, but rarely declined when someone produced a vial of cocaine. Joe smoked a lot of pot, and I regularly carried gallons of water out to his marijuana patch.

After Jed joined the staff of *Quest*, it wasn't long before I was brought on as a part-time contributing editor. Funded by Garner Ted Armstrong's Worldwide Church of God, the magazine was to be a celebration of excellence. Everyone was skeptical going in, but when Robert Shnayerson, the former editor of *Harper's*, was promised full autonomy, we settled into *Quest*'s upscale offices. Since it was cozy, cheap, and available, Jed also settled into my old apartment.

In 1979, the same year my father won the National Book Award for *The Snow Leopard*, I secured an entry-level editorial job at Penguin Books. The timing couldn't have been more fortuitous, since I wanted to move on from the *Paris Review*, and *Quest*'s death knell was sounded when the Church installed one of its officials in a corner office.

With my arrival at Penguin I believed I had achieved genuine legitimacy, parental pull notwithstanding. Dick Seaver, my mother's old friend and colleague, was the editorial director, and my newest mentor. Tom Guinzburg, a childhood friend of my father's, was editor in chief at Viking Press, Penguin's sister company and my father's nonfiction publisher.

"I saved your life once," Tom said as we stood in the hall one afternoon. "You couldn't have been more than two and were being washed out to sea by a pretty strong undertow when you came up against my leg. I reached down and hauled you out."

Things went well at Penguin for the next two years. Happy in my work, I was promoted to associate editor and given, for the first time, my own small office. But as much as I savored that achievement, I was beginning to fear that my success wouldn't last.

Clamming with my father had become an annual tradition, and we arranged another rendezvous in the summer of 1980. Because Lisa had drunkenly flirted with him earlier that year, embarrassing everyone and prompting Maria and me to ponder a homicide, I thought it best to go alone. The Land Rover had finally given out, and we agreed that I would pick him up before continuing on to Sag Harbor.

The clams were all but farmed out at our old spot, so we took his boat to a bed he had discovered on the lee side of an island off the Northwest Woods. A Carolina fishing vessel he had christened *Wind Bird*, its large open deck gave it the appearance of a miniature tug. Even with this advantage our take was steadily decreasing, but that didn't lessen the pleasure of being on the water. We generally worked separately, left to our own thoughts. When he called my attention to an osprey returning to its large nest, its wings stretched against high cloud, I was grateful to have seen it.

On the way back to Sagaponack I stopped at an intersection before making a right turn. Looking left, I swung into the road and a car horn screamed in my ear. My father grabbed the wheel and jerked it sharply to the right. Its horn still blaring, the other car swerved into the oncoming lane.

"Pull over," he commanded.

I eased on to the shoulder and stopped. Neither of us said a word for several seconds, and he let his hand fall from the dashboard. A steady stream of traffic passed from both directions as my pulse began to race. Speaking in a measured undertone, he asked, "Did you see that car?"

I stared straight ahead, breathing rapidly. "No," I confessed at last. He let out a deep sigh.

"Luke, it isn't safe for you to keep driving. You need to stop at once. I'll take you back to Springs." I kept silent, as if an internal battery had finally gone dead. After a long pause he placed a hand on my arm and said, "I'm sorry, but we need to switch seats."

My parents and I had a brief conference in my mother's driveway, during which I surrendered to objective reality and promised never to drive again. When my mother returned from Sagaponack, we moved to the deck to speak privately. "It breaks my heart, Luke, but it's the right decision," she said. She looked at me with love and compassion, and I thought I could detect a residual trace of helpless guilt.

I nodded but didn't respond, wishing I were alone. Jackie and my sister laughed together inside the house, Lisa struggling to join their conversation. "Thank God I'm normal," Jackie almost shouted, and I couldn't help but smile. Fully "out" by this time, he was funnier than ever.

After almost a minute my mother said she was worried about

me. I replied that I was all right, that this day had to come sooner or later. Stressing that she would help in whatever way she could, she asked whether we might discuss another concern, and I nodded again. "Are you happy? I mean, with Lisa?"

Like the rest of my family and most of my friends, she saw my marriage as an unfortunate mistake. While not yet clear to me, others had known from the start that the match would turn out badly. Before I could respond Lisa came out to join us, a drink in hand. "Look what I've got for you, honey," she said.

Unbeknownst to us, we were caught up in a vortex of alcoholism, our partnership centered around drinking. While we worked, saw friends and family, and otherwise appeared to be a normal young couple, alcohol was directing our lives far more than either of us realized. From the beginning it was the glue of our relationship, and soon became the filter through which everything was communicated. We drank every night, never socialized without alcohol, and began to pull away from people who didn't drink like we did.

One night in the White Horse a man approached and identified himself as a police detective. "I know who you are," he said. "We almost had you back then on Bank Street. You know what I'm talking about. I know you do." I said nothing as I moved away, still with no inkling that I might be living on borrowed time.

Lisa and I never spoke about my worsening vision, since her denial was on a par with my own, and I was becoming more sullen and withdrawn. I felt progressively trapped and alone as my eyesight deteriorated, sought escape in alcohol with increasing intensity, and the downward spiral soon accelerated beyond my ability to control it.

By my twenty-eighth birthday I was drinking a quart of vodka each day, and an unrelenting chorus of self-denunciation, not unlike that often experienced by paranoid schizophrenics, was my constant waking companion. *You're no good. You're a fool, a fake, and everyone knows it. You're a piece of shit, worthless. Who do you think you are?* These thoughts became gospel, absolute truths which dictated everything I did. If anyone ever saw beyond my increasingly fragile exterior, I was convinced they would find emptiness, a vacuum without substance. The only time I experienced any relief was when drinking, and preferably drinking alone. I began to shut Lisa out, speaking less and less, often snapping at her when I did. When one night she asked why I drank so much, I countered with her own drinking, and the discussion ended there.

My work was suffering significantly by the middle of my third year at Penguin. Still diligent about arriving on time, I was having trouble concentrating and started to make serious mistakes. Because I couldn't cover up or otherwise compensate for the more egregious blunders, they didn't go unnoticed. I began to put on weight, the telltale bloat and facial puffiness of the alcoholic.

It was also becoming more difficult to read. Whether the result of too much drink or the progression of RP, or both, I struggled to keep up. Kathryn Court, who succeeded Dick after he left to become editor in chief at Holt, Rinehart and Winston, began to confront me on my poor performance. She asked whether I needed help of any kind, simultaneously insisting that things needed to improve.

An annual physical revealed that my liver enzymes were elevated, and my doctor, Eric Andreae, asked how much I drank. I replied that everyone in publishing drank too much, hoping he would find this funny. Instead, he raised the specter of serious liver damage if I didn't cut down. Promising to comply, I was relieved he hadn't asked me to stop.

In the fall of 1981, I took Michael Arlen to lunch. Then the television critic for the *New Yorker*, he was also the author of several books for which I had acquired the paperback rights. As usual, I drank too much and, full of boozy bluster, suggested he abandon Farrar, Straus and Giroux, his hardcover publisher. "I'm sure we can do better for you at Viking-Penguin, Michael," I promised, having no basis for this, or any real idea of how such negotiations were actually conducted. By the time we parted I was certain I had fully redeemed myself.

Kathryn called me into her office the next morning. "I have received a complaint from Roger Straus." Pausing, she asked, "Did you suggest to Michael Arlen that he should come over to us?"

"Yes, I did. I thought it would be good for everyone."

"What gave you the idea that you had the authority to do such a thing?" She asked sharply, her words like arrows.

"I'm sorry if I did anything wrong," I said, beginning to sense what was coming.

"Roger was irate," she continued, "and I don't blame him. I managed to smooth things over in the end, but Arlen will not be coming here."

My double-breasted blazer was tight under my arms and around my waist as I sat on her sofa. It was the only jacket which still fit me, but it no longer concealed my swelling belly. Sweat began to break out on my forehead. "I'm sorry if I overstepped my bounds, Kathryn," I said. "I didn't mean to embarrass you."

"Luke, this can't go on. I've tried to help you, given you plenty of time to turn things around, but it hasn't gotten any better. Now this thing with Farrar, Straus. It just can't be overlooked." She paused before concluding, "I'm afraid we need to let you go. I'm sorry. This wasn't an easy decision, but I just don't see any alternative. I wish the best for you and, well, there really isn't anything else to say."

"So this is my last day, you mean?" I asked.

"Yes," she replied. Stunned, I left immediately, without saying goodbye to anyone.

Initially anxious about my future and how I would support myself, a deep calm had sublimated all fear before I got home. That I no longer had to live in dread of being "found out" or humiliated over my increasing incompetence felt like a liberation. That night neither Lisa nor I was particularly worried, since she still worked, and we were certain I would soon find another job. It never occurred to either of us that this was already an impossibility.

"What are you doing?" Lisa asked two months later. She had glimpsed my hand sliding a glass under the sofa as she emerged from the bedroom. "Are you drinking? Jesus, it's only seven o'clock."

I had awakened an hour earlier, relieved I hadn't wet the bed. Getting up slowly, I picked up my "nightcap" and closed the bedroom door behind me. Grabbing a second glass on my way to the living room, I sat on the sofa and cracked the shutters, certain I could look out without being seen. No fresh snow had fallen. A car rumbled over the cobblestones of West 12th Street, and an elderly man passed with his small dog. A dark morning, filthy ridges of snow lined the curb.

The previous night's drink was rancid, but I wasn't going to waste that much vodka. Within minutes I felt the urge to vomit, and did so into the second glass. This over, I knew the rest would stay down.

When Lisa confronted me, I was on my second drink. Eager to please, I made her a cup of coffee and some toast. "Listen," I began, "I promise this won't last. I just need to find another job. I know I haven't been looking that hard lately, but I promise, I swear, things will get better very soon."

"Luke. How much more time do you need to get it together? Do you really want to? Maybe you've gotten just a little too comfortable with my taking care of everything?"

"No," I protested. "Of course not. You'll see, I promise." Within a week I was making no effort to hide the morning drink. If she objected I lashed out with vociferous abuse, and afterward we often didn't speak before she left for work.

By ten o'clock I'd had enough to settle my nerves and was usually ready for my daily sojourn. The only purpose of this outing was to buy cigarettes and vodka, to make sure I had enough of both to get me through not just that day, but the following morning as well. It was essential I not run out before the liquor stores opened at ten. To be assured of an adequate supply I was buying half-gallons of the bottom-shelf stuff every day.

I went out in sneakers without socks, sweatpants without enough elastic in the waist and a battered Chesterfield coat. I had neither showered nor shaved, and might not have brushed my teeth. Since there were three liquor stores within a four-block radius, I was careful to maintain a fixed rotation. That way, I believed, none of the shopkeepers would have any reason to suspect I was an alcoholic.

Safely home with my provisions, I hoped I wouldn't get any calls or alarming mail. If there were reruns on television I hadn't seen and no one rang the doorbell, I was especially content. I watched television all day, occasionally passing out or reading a few pages of Stephen King or Raymond Chandler, simple narratives which didn't require too much concentration. Hiding behind the partially open shutters, I languished in my increasingly brittle cocoon. It took more and more alcohol to keep the terrors at bay, and sometimes oblivion was my only refuge. As the weeks wore on I began to have trouble following the thin TV plots, and no longer attempted to read anything. More often than not, I ate only when Lisa came home and made dinner.

Concerned about my well-being after I was fired from Penguin, my father offered to subsidize a round of therapy. I started seeing a Reichian on the Upper West Side, but dreaded the sessions because they required that I venture out into the real world. I had to wash up beforehand, put on at least a semblance of decent clothing, ride the subway uptown and, most difficult, restrict my morning drinking to a level which would stop the shakes without getting me too drunk. I was never so relieved as when I returned home from therapy, secure in the knowledge that I had a full week's respite.

One day my father called and asked to accompany me to my next session. Probably to ensure my compliance, he insisted on picking me up. By the time he rang the bell, I'd had a few drinks but didn't think I was obviously intoxicated.

When we arrived uptown, he faced the therapist. "How can you accept your fee when Luke is doing so poorly? Haven't you been addressing his problems? Look at him. Hasn't it struck you that something is very wrong?"

The therapist reluctantly acknowledged that he might not have been paying sufficient attention to my current situation, and my father informed him that I wouldn't be returning.

Sharing a cab that would drop him on the East Side before taking me home, he told me that he was off to Japan for a Zen retreat. "I'm worried about you, Lucassin," he said. To my surprise, there was no hint of disappointment or potential recrimination. "Watch it, or you might become an alcoholic."

Riding downtown, I was filled with love for him, but also a certain melancholy. I had minimized my drinking, and this evasion exacerbated the guilt I still felt about betraying his confidence four years earlier. No longer deceiving myself entirely, his warning struck me as both ironic and naive, another indicator of how far apart we really were.

While I didn't make the connection at the time, Lisa had called him to express her growing concern. Unbeknownst to me, she had also contacted my mother, Jackie, and other friends, and they all began to show up. Everyone expressed their love, but most stopped short of identifying my drinking as a serious problem. No one wanted to see me as a chronic alcoholic, and most were probably wary of unleashing my anger. I assured everyone that I would be all right once I dealt with a few things and got back to work, and this seemed to satisfy them. But as soon as the door closed on one of my visitors, I pulled the glass out from its hiding place and retreated to the sofa. My drinking escalated to the point where I was in a full or partial blackout most of the time. It took on a frantic, almost desperate quality, as if my life depended on consuming as much alcohol as possible, and even a moment's clarity was too terrible to contemplate.

With the approach of my twenty-ninth birthday, I began to notice traces of blood in my urine. In the harsh light of the morning bathroom, the reddish tint almost glowed in the dull white of the toilet. When this deepened to scarlet, I was alarmed enough to show Lisa, and she pleaded with me to get help. "Christ, it looks like the My Lai massacre," I muttered.

More unsettling than these small blood baths was the unacknowledged certainty that they were related to my drinking. That I might need to stop was unthinkable, something to be avoided at all costs. Terrified, it didn't take long to convince myself that I didn't have a liver, so the bleeding couldn't be the result of my drinking. It was a symptom of some other problem, something I would get checked out at some point, but I didn't need to stop. Years later I would learn that being so out of touch with reality is the hallmark of psychosis.

As I looked out the window one morning, before lapsing into the first blackout of the day, I watched people going to work, children laughing with their parents on the way to school, and my neighbor whistling as he descended the stairs. Suddenly I was convinced that I had lost the capacity to love. For the first time I was horrified not by the prospect of life without alcohol, but by what had happened to me. I had never felt so alienated, so emotionally deadened. At that moment I saw no hope for redemption and feared that I was irrevocably cut off from any real connection to the world.

Whether prompted by the unimaginable loneliness of that vision or, like a good military tactician, sensing that I needed to give some ground in order to regroup, I called Dr. Andreae. All I said to him, he recounted later, was, "You have to help me get off the sauce."

I arrived at his office the next day, having plied myself with enough vodka to get uptown. When I sat across from him, Dr. Andreae said, "You need to go to the hospital."

"I don't want to hear that," I replied. "That's not an option."

We moved to the examining room, and he palpated my liver. "You need to go to the hospital today," he said calmly.

"No," I snapped, cutting him off. Jabbing a finger in his face, I countered, "What *you* need to do is give me something to help me stop drinking. No more talk about going into the hospital, because it's not happening, today or any other day. I want a pill, something to help me relax so I won't need to drink so much."

Probably realizing that any attempt at persuasion would be useless, he gave me a prescription for Librium. Thanking him, I went home and filled the script immediately. After taking twice the recommended dose I decided that it wouldn't work and went out to get my usual half gallon.

But something had let go, and the next morning I called to say I would do whatever he recommended.

While I continued to drink as much as I could, plans were being made to get me into St. Luke's hospital. Lisa was cautioned against removing the vodka, since alcohol withdrawal could result in seizure, or even death. For the next few days I remained calm, letting others take control. Only dimly aware of how I had gotten there, I was injected with a high dose of Valium as soon as I entered St. Luke's. I hadn't returned from Oxford, but I was back in Morningside Heights.

Eight

BEFORE RETURNING TO BED I STOOD BRIEFLY AT THE WINDOW, soothed by how the snow seemed to hold the world in perfect stillness. As I looked out across the trees, their bare branches outlined in white against the April sky, it seemed that New York had paused for breath, its pulse somehow suspended. Unnatural in the city scape, the white was still unsullied by the grit beneath. It must have been snowing on the way to the hospital, but I had no memory of traveling uptown in the blizzard.

Pulling back from the window, I reached out for the bed. I hadn't bothered to put on the plastic slippers, and didn't much care if the loosely closed gown revealed my backside to passersby. My roommate, an older Greek man, was silent behind the curtain which separated us. I couldn't remember whether we had greeted one another when I was admitted, but we didn't speak now.

The nurse arrived right on schedule. "Be sure to take all of these," she said. "You need your vitamins as much as the other medication. We have to build up your strength."

Thanking her, I quickly confirmed that the two-toned Librium capsule nested among the other pills in the small paper container. Over the past two days I had deduced that the precious

111

cup arrived every four hours. Now I counted the time between doses, my anxiety rising if the little tray arrived even a minute late. Once I had taken all the pills, calm was restored and I set-tled back into the routine of hospital life—the tranquilizing cycle of meals, regular visits by the nurses, the doctors making their rounds, napping, and the assurance that I didn't need to do or decide anything. As long as I got the Librium regularly, noth-ing disturbed me.

Dr. Andreae appeared, chart in hand. After we exchanged pleasantries he began to expatiate on the state of my health. "On a scale of one to fifteen," he said in summation, "your cirrhosis is at a three."

In a perfect illustration of "intellectualization," the unconscious defense mechanism in which thinking is used to stave off emotion, I was struck not by the diagnosis, but his math. Why hadn't he said, "On a scale of one to five, your cirrhosis is at a one?" Perhaps it was because he was French, I decided. Looking out the window at the treetops, I was glad to see the snow again. Maybe it was almost medication time.

"You should consider a number of things regarding your future," he went on, but I wasn't paying much attention. He said something about remaining in the hospital for a week, that it was important to be fully detoxed, and that I should think about what steps I needed to take to prevent relapse. I nodded vaguely, saying nothing, not particularly alarmed about anything. But when he recommended a twenty-eight-day inpatient program to address my "alcoholism," he got my attention.

Sitting up as much as I could, I said, "Doctor, there is no way I can go away for a month. My life is a shambles. I need to get a job, save my marriage, and get myself back out there. I can't hide away for a month. It's just not an option."

He paused for some time before responding. "Lucas, look at yourself. You talk about finding work, but you can't even get on a subway. How are you going to get a job, or hope to hold one if you drink again?"

His bluntness was like a body blow. He was right, and I knew it. I could barely walk, much less commute to work. Dr. Andreae had explained that I was suffering from peripheral neuropathy, a numbing of the hands and feet brought on by chronic alcoholism. Although I was only twenty-eight, I shuffled like an old man. He continued his assault on my denial, parrying every objection with reminders of the damage my drinking had done and stressing that I had no hope of restoring anything I valued unless I stayed sober. At last he concluded, "Based on the tests we have run, it is safe to say that you will be dead within six months if you keep drinking."

Still not fully appreciating the gravity of his message, and doing my best to keep it at bay, I replied, "Okay, Doctor. I get it. I can't drink anymore. I really do understand. I'll stay here for a week, but I can't go away for a month. I just can't. I need to get my life back together."

Without pausing, Dr. Andreae looked straight at me and replied, "If you return home after a week here, you'll be drunk in an hour."

Looking to the trees for deliverance, I kept silent. Something inside gave way, another layer of resistance, and there was no hope of retrieving it. I didn't believe I was an alcoholic, but couldn't deny that his prediction was accurate. "All right, I'll do it your way. Whatever you say," I almost whispered. Hearing this second surrender, Dr. Andreae moved to the phone and reserved a bed at the Smithers Alcoholism Center, leaving me no chance to mull it over.

My week in the hospital passed like a slow-moving river, the time marked by medication dosings. I had no thought of canceling the rehab reservation, my dread at that prospect sufficiently dulled by the Librium. Without the strength to put up a real fight, I was at least guaranteed a few more days of peace. Visitors came and went, their presence forgotten in a sedative haze almost as soon as they departed. By the fourth day the snow was melting rapidly, and dirty tracks had been etched into the sooty whiteness.

A nurse came in and announced that a "Mr. Davis" was waiting in the visitor's lounge. It took me a few moments to realize that this must be Paul Davis, whom I didn't know well and hadn't been expecting. Putting on a robe and the hospital slippers, I shuffled down the hall. Warm sunlight flooded the corridor, a sign that spring had finally arrived.

Paul sat alone on a sofa across from the door, and we smiled at one another before I entered the room. After we moved to a far corner, away from the relentless droning of hospital announcements, Paul began to recount his own struggles with alcohol. He noted that he had been sober for a number of years, relating his story quietly, without drama. By the time he finished, the shame I had felt at seeing him had vanished. Now certain I wouldn't be judged, I poured out my own tale, and he listened with genuine interest. Before long we were laughing at some of the more outlandish details of our histories, the humor borne out of shared trust and mutual acceptance.

Paul's visit was a tremendous gift. For the first time I was sure I wasn't alone, that there was at least one other person who understood. Hearing that he had abstained from alcohol for so long, something I couldn't imagine, gave me badly needed hope. Most important, Paul was proof that life without booze was not just possible, but might even be worth living.

Ignoring the mandate that new patients be off all detox medication for at least twenty-four hours, Dr. Andreae slipped me one last Librium shortly before I left for rehab and wished me well. The building on East 97th Street which housed Smithers had once belonged to Billy Rose, the 1940s Broadway impresario and composer. The mansion, as it was commonly called, still showed signs of its former grandeur, with a sweeping staircase, marble floors, intricately carved pillars, brass plumbing fixtures, and a large patio.

This covered a pool which Rose had built for his second wife, Eleanor Holm, an Olympic swimmer.

Despite my secretly sedated condition, I began to shake and sweat as soon as I passed through the wrought iron doors. During my intake the nurse wondered whether I had really come straight from the hospital, insinuating that I might have stopped at a liquor store on the way. When I denied having done anything untoward, she asked why I was in such a distressed state. "If you don't know," I replied, "maybe I'm in the wrong place." Because my blood pressure was precariously high, the staff were reluctant to admit me. Afraid I might be in withdrawal, they were wary of a possible seizure and weren't at all sure they could manage my hypertension.

I finally convinced them that what they were seeing was nothing more than the outward manifestations of abject fear. Confronting a future without alcohol, or drugs of any kind, I was terrified. I had dreaded this moment for months, convinced I probably couldn't survive a life of unaltered reality. At last they agreed to admit me, but only on condition that my blood pressure quickly return to normal. If it didn't, they would have no choice but to refer me back to the hospital.

When everything was settled, I was shown to my room. None of my three roommates was present, and I was left alone for a few minutes before lunch was announced. Sitting on my bed, I wondered how it had come to this. How had I gotten here? Had I really lost control of my life so entirely? I had no idea what to do, or even if I had any choice. It seemed that everything was out of my hands, that others were making all the decisions, and I had no power to resist.

My legs shook so badly in the lunch line that a man approached and asked whether I needed to sit down. Introducing himself as "Vic," he took my arm. Short and almost gaunt, Vic had pointed features and a ferret's eyes. I assured him that I would be all right, that I was just a little anxious, but he stayed by me as the line moved forward. Sunlight came in through the French doors which opened onto the patio, and spirited conversation competed with the clatter of trays and silverware. I suppressed a groan when I saw what was being served.

Taking my elbow as we moved toward an empty table, Vic urged me to sit while he retrieved his own tray. Looking down at my plate, I decided to leave the peas for last. Maybe my hands would stop shaking if I waited long enough. Vic told me that this was his second time in Smithers, adding that he had been through thirty detoxes and six rehabs. He was only thirty-five. As I had feared, all the peas jumped from my fork when I finally attempted to eat them, but Vic promised that everything would get better.

Despite my tremulous start, it didn't take long to get acclimated to the rhythms of rehab life. Highly regimented, the day was divided into various group and individual therapy sessions, didactic lectures and, in the evening, a support group led by an outside speaker. As interesting as their stories were, it annoyed me that everyone introduced themselves as a "grateful recovering alcoholic." Effectively locked in a gilded cage, my life a catastrophe, I resented the implication that I should somehow be thankful.

One of my roommates was the loudest snorer I'd ever heard, but he wasn't the only reason I didn't sleep. When I complained about my insomnia to the nurse, vainly hoping for a sleeping pill, she explained that my body was undergoing significant metabolic adjustments. My system was used to a great deal of alcohol, and it would take some time to restore a natural equilibrium. "No one ever died from lack of sleep," I heard again and again, but I had my doubts after the third night. I don't know whether exhaustion contributed to the gradual lowering of my blood pressure, which was checked four times a day, but it finally returned to acceptable levels and I began to sleep.

Patients came and went at all times. Since I was so often at the nurses' station, which abutted the front entrance, I was repeatedly struck by the ambivalence of those about to leave. They had all spoken of how they couldn't wait to go, couldn't wait to do this or that. But always hesitated when the big moment arrived. There was someone they hadn't said goodbye to, or another who had neglected to give them their phone number. "I'd be out that door like a shot," I thought. Weeks later, when it was my turn, I understood why everyone paused at the threshold.

"I used to drive my husband crazy," Kathy said in group. "He could never figure out where I hid the vodka. I'd cook dinner, we'd sit down in the dining room and I'd go back in the kitchen to do the dishes. When I came out with booze on my breath, half in the bag, he'd rush in and turn the kitchen upside down, but he never found it."

"Where was it?" someone asked.

"In the Windex bottle under the sink," she replied. "I would fill it with vodka and add just the right amount of blue food coloring. It worked like a charm, but I guess I really wasn't fooling anyone."

Marveling at her ingenuity, we all had a good laugh. Bob Williams, one of the counselors, turned to me. "Luke, why don't you tell your story to the group today?"

I was a week into treatment and had learned that this wasn't the end of the rehab road for any of us. We would all receive one of three "aftercare" recommendations: a referral to Hazelden in Minnesota for another twenty-eight days followed by a three-month stay at a "halfway" house; a referral directly to a halfway house; or, by far the most desirable, outpatient care in New York. Upon hearing this, everything I said and did was geared toward securing the "easiest" recommendation, and telling my story was no exception. I related my entire history with alcohol, omitting nothing. I was open and honest, two traits I had learned were most desirable to the staff, and played it to the hilt.

When I finished, everyone commended me on my candor, and someone suggested that I had broken through my denial. Pleased, I thanked them for their support, stressing that I couldn't have done it without their help.

Thumbing through the pages on his clipboard, Bob said, "Nice job, Luke, but what about Valium? I didn't hear you mention that." Compact and quietly self-assured, Bob's voice had the power of an oracle, and trying to fool or manipulate him was useless.

"Well, yes, I did take Valium, but only by prescription," I replied, confident I had dodged his bullet.

"How long did you have the prescription?" he asked.

"Let's see," I replied. "About ten years, I think."

"Did you ever let it lapse?"

"Well, no, I never did."

Unbeknownst to me, his clipboard held the information I had given on the day I arrived. Among other things, it listed not only every drug I had ever taken, but how much and for how long. I didn't remember filling it out and cringed as Bob went on. "And LSD?"

"Well, yes, I did that too."

"And marijuana? Heroin? Cocaine? Barbiturates? Amphetamines?" As he ticked off each one, I was required to give the group a brief summary of my usage and how it had affected me. By the time he was done they had a very different perspective on how much I had actually progressed. "Thanks, Luke," Bob concluded. "That was very informative."

After Lisa arrived for a weekend visit with alcohol on her breath, the staff asked that she not return. She was more relieved than offended, and neither of us protested the decision. My mother, Mike, and Maria came on Family Day. They were shown a film in which an alcoholic adman regularly asks his wife to call his boss with a plausible excuse for not coming to work. The wife finally threatens to throw him out, and he stops drinking for several months. When he relapses and again asks her to call the boss, she hands him the phone and tells him to make the call himself. Mike left immediately after the screening, declaring that he "couldn't stand it."

"Which one do you sympathize with?" Renee Zito, my counselor, asked the assembled. She had an ironic temperament, a pixie haircut, and enormous breasts. "The husband or the wife?" Maria picked the wife and my mother the drunk.

As part of my strategy to secure an outpatient aftercare recommendation, I read much more than was required and devoted many pages to every written assignment. I laid on the guilt and shame about how I had hurt others and violated myself, mainly because this was what I thought the staff wanted to hear. Still not fully convinced I was an alcoholic, I was curious to know how I might have become one, and repeatedly sought enlightenment from Renee.

"You know," she said in one of our sessions, "you ask a lot of questions, and that's a good thing. But there's one question which, in asking all the others, you seem to be systematically avoiding, and that question is, 'How do I get better?'"

Although I didn't acknowledge it then, that got through to me. I saw in an instant how, by focusing on my life before drinking, I was continuing to sidestep taking a hard look at what I needed to change.

"I've been thinking about my future, Renee," I said a few days later. "I think I might like to become a counselor. A great idea, right?"

"Tell you what," she replied. "You stay sober for about four years and we'll talk, but you should put that out of your mind for now."

"All right," I said, chastened. "I get it, but I won't forget."

Because she knew I would be perfectly content to spend my last two weeks reading and writing, Renee declared that my only assignment from then on was to be with people. Nothing more, just be with people. Sitting up straight, I protested that I had a lot of unfinished homework. She told me not to worry and ended our session. Getting closer to others—and allowing them to get closer to me—turned out to be the most difficult assignment of all.

In my last week I was summoned to the nurse's station late one evening. A man with a large suitcase, a florid face, and a hugely distended belly stood by the desk, and I could see at once that he was drunk. The nurse introduced us and asked me to show him up to our room. As we mounted the staircase he informed me that he was a colonel in the Army and an expert on alcoholism. Patting his stomach, he said it was his liver and laughed heartily. Given my recent diagnosis, I didn't think this funny and thoroughly disliked him by the time we got to our room.

The next morning he interrupted Renee's lecture to correct her on a statistical point, and my antipathy intensified. That afternoon, in community meeting, the staff asked whether anyone had a concern they would like to voice. Up went my hand and, in front of everyone, I eviscerated him. With much self-righteous indignation I denounced his arriving drunk (conveniently forgetting that last Librium), his arrogance, how he presumptuously corrected "my" counselor, and the hypocrisy of presenting himself as an expert when there he sat, a patient, like the rest of us. Since we were always encouraged to air our feelings, I was sure I had done the right thing by not bottling up my anger.

Renee signaled to me as I left the room. "That was interesting," she said.

Pausing for a moment, she asked, "Now, what is it about him that reminds you of yourself?" I was flabbergasted. How could she compare him to me at all, on any level? Not just blindsided, I felt deeply betrayed, and then it hit me. I was often just as boastful and opinionated when drunk, and it wasn't a pretty picture. While I never became friends with "the general," as he came to be known, I did apologize to him.

"You are so arrogant, so stubborn," Renee said at the close of our last session, "that I wouldn't worry about when you're feeling bad, because you'll just bull your way through it. But I'd worry about when you're feeling good."

I was scheduled to leave the next day. Like those before me, I couldn't wait to go. Shielded from the world for five weeks, I longed for freedom and a shot at redemption. I had received the coveted recommendation for outpatient aftercare, but later learned that it wasn't because of my stratagems. Slated to go to Hazelden from the outset, the change was made in my last days, when I finally abandoned all attempts at deceiving the staff. Nevertheless, because I shared more traits with the general than I cared to admit, I didn't pay much attention to Renee's parting words.

The cab ride downtown underscored why my own hesitation at the door was well founded. On every block, it seemed, there was a bar, a liquor store, or a deli that sold beer. A bus went by with a vodka ad plastered to its side, and I began to appreciate how vulnerable I really was. Alcohol was in the house when I arrived, but I didn't think I had the right to ask Lisa to throw it out. Booze was all around me and always would be, and it was up to me not to succumb to its Circean charms.

All the liquor was on the marble-topped bar when I arrived in Springs the next day, but that night I got to a meeting at the tiny Episcopalian church. The group was a perfect cross section of the community, from an extremely wealthy woman to a local bayman still struggling to make a living. To my dismay, the format was a "round robin," so I had to say something when my turn came. My voice rising at least a full octave, I stammered, "My name is Luke and this is my first meeting outside of rehab." When everyone applauded, I couldn't hold back the tears. Once again, I was more relieved than humiliated, certain that I had been understood and accepted.

I continued to follow all treatment recommendations over the next two weeks, attending aftercare, reading the suggested literature, and going to my local support group at least once a day.

When a stranger offered to be my sponsor, someone I could call for guidance, I accepted at once. In addition to taking the first steps toward finding work, I began to jog around the neighborhood, thrilled to be exercising for the first time in years.

Memorial Day weekend of 1982 ushered in the first tropical weather of that summer, and I was convinced that jogging in the heat would accelerate the release of toxins from my body. As difficult as it was for one so out of shape, just knowing that I was engaged in something so healthful inspired me to keep going. My appearance probably confirming that I was in no condition to run in such weather, passersby sometimes leaned toward me and said, "Mister, it's too hot. You really shouldn't be out here." Mine was a two-mile route on Greenwich Street, from 12th down to Chambers and back, and my goal was to complete it without stopping to walk. I was hitting a wall on the return leg one afternoon when a thunderstorm unleashed a deluge. Instantly energized, I let out an exhilarated howl and sprinted the last half mile.

The sun had returned by the time I showered, and I went out for a walk. With hardly a pause, I strolled into one of my old liquor stores as if I'd never broken the cycle. The shopkeeper reached for the bottom-shelf vodka, I gave him the exact change—six dollars and thirty cents—and neither of us said a word. Walking home with the bottle cradled in my arm, I knew I would finish it, so there was no sense in pretending otherwise. After all I'd been through, all I'd learned, I never considered getting to a meeting or calling anyone.

I woke in a sweat. That I had relapsed so easily shook me even more than the after-effects of the vodka. Stripped of all defenses, I was raw. Not at all sure I could stop again, I feared I'd lost everything and called Renee.

"Well, I can't say I'm surprised," she began. "Let's hope you get something out of this, that your appreciation of alcoholism shifts from your head to your gut. That's my hope, but we'll see."

"How will I know?" I asked.

"You'll know by how you feel," she replied.

"What I feel right now is scared," I said.

"A little fear can be a good thing. Maybe one day you'll experience the serenity which comes with acceptance." I thanked her, feeling anything but serene as we hung up.

Minutes later the doorbell rang and Mike's friend, the writer Erje Ayden, stood outside. He said he had been sent to "check up" on me. We sat on my stoop, and I blurted out what had happened. Erje, who had also been a friend of Frank's, smiled and said that he, too, was in the program, and it was okay if I drank every three or four days. Even my muddled brain knew this wasn't exactly true, but I said nothing.

Erje attempted to reassure me as best he could, sincerely hoping to help. Then he asked if I had some money, because he wanted a beer and didn't have any cash. I gave him a few dollars and he went to the deli around the corner. Returning with two large cans, he offered me one. When I declined, he proceeded to drink them both. Since I liked his company and didn't care to be inside with Lisa, who was upset over my relapse, I stayed with him. She refused to let him use the bathroom, so he urinated in the street before departing. As soon as he was gone I rushed to a meeting. "Is anyone counting days?" the chairman asked.

With my heart pounding, I raised my hand and said, "My name is Luke and I'm an alcoholic. This is my first day back." I knew they had been following my progress and was sure I had let them down. I had failed and would now be seen as a pariah, a threat to everyone's recovery. I actually expected the chairman to stop the meeting and ask me to leave, having no idea at the time that this was just another reflection of my grandiosity. That group also broke into applause, and I haven't taken a drink since.

As soon as I returned from rehab it was obvious that my marriage to Lisa was in serious jeopardy. She continued to drink heavily, and the extent to which our union had been based on mutual imbibing became progressively clearer. When I stopped there was little to bind us, little else we shared. After my relapse I spent more time at meetings, and she became increasingly jealous.

"Why do you need to be with those people so often? What about me? I put up with all your bullshit only to have you disappear now that you're sober? It's not fair." I tried to explain that the meetings—and those people—were crucial to my recovery, that I didn't stand a chance at anything if I didn't stay sober. I stressed that our marriage wouldn't survive if I drank again, not yet realizing that the opposite was far closer to the truth. She wanted none of it, and the gulf between us continued to widen as the weeks passed.

Lisa had good reason to be suspicious. I was forging close friendships in my group and soon preferred their company to hers, especially when she was drinking. Although some members had colorful nicknames, such as "Stan the Hat," "Shoeless John," "Hands-On Susan," and "Jimmy the Worm," the intimacy which typified the meetings fostered powerful bonds. That the room was small and barely lit, its dark green walls encasing a perpetual cloud of cigarette smoke, also contributed to an atmosphere of closeness, warmth, and security. It was a refuge from the world outside, a place of comfortable respite, not unlike that drawn by Dickens in his depictions of rural English pubs. I felt bad for Lisa, but her reluctance to stop drinking represented a threat to our marriage as powerful as my refusal to start again.

The tension between us continued to mount until one night, about three months after my relapse, she said, "You know, I liked you better when you were drinking." At that moment, unless she was willing to stop, I knew our marriage was over. Her drinking had worsened since I'd gotten sober, and I realized it would be almost impossible to remain together unless one of us gave in. The next morning I asked her to get help but she refused. Our life together devolved into a pattern of coexistence, with almost no pretense at being close, far less intimate.

Getting fired from Penguin had devastated me, and securing another position in publishing, the only means by which I believed I might restore some dignity, became an obsession. I started a log which eventually listed every publishing house in New York, when I had sent a résumé and to whom, when I had made a follow-up call, whether I had spoken to someone, whether an interview had been scheduled, and when I should call back. Months went by without success, and I began to fear that my reputation had been irreparably tarnished.

I was also attempting to mend relationships damaged by my drinking, but wasn't always welcomed with open arms. For the most part, family, friends, and acquaintances were glad I had stopped and grateful to have past hurts acknowledged. Even if forgiveness wasn't entirely forthcoming, everyone wished me well. It was especially difficult to write Roger Straus. In a long, single-spaced letter I confessed to my problem with alcohol, offering this more as an explanation than an excuse, and apologized for having compromised his relationship with Michael Arlen. Roger's response arrived shortly thereafter. Thanking me for my letter, he praised my courage in taking steps to turn my life around and assured me that no real damage had been done. Not just gracious, his note was kind and generous. It arrived in a large padded envelope, accompanied by two books of poetry he thought I might enjoy.

Along with sending out résumés and making calls to potential employers, I began to do some freelance editing to earn a little money and keep hope alive. I knew it was important to get that oar back in the water, to flex my editorial muscle in whatever way I could. Cobbling a number of small jobs together, I worked as a reader for two paperback houses, wrote a few reviews, and edited articles for various psychiatric and psychological publications. My father asked me to assist in the editing of *Indian Country*, a compilation of magazine articles he had written on different native peoples. He rejected most of my revisions, but accepted my suggestions on how they should be ordered.

Although frustrated by my inability to find a full-time job, I became aware of a gradual shift. After several months the urgency I had attached to getting back with a major house was diminishing. While some of this may have been due to circumstance, my embryonic resignation also signaled the beginnings of significant healing. I was starting to feel better about myself, my identity and worth no longer linked exclusively to vocation. In spite of my innate tendencies, I had finally managed to integrate a little humility and acceptance into my outlook on life.

Having established a foundation of sobriety, I began to feel the need for more structure and a steady income. With no other prospects, I returned to the Strand bookstore, where I had worked after my sophomore year in college. A quick look around told me that not much had changed. The forty-eight-cent carts were still out front, red signs still adorned the pillars, and dust covered everything. I was hired and told to report to work the next day. Fighting off a lingering sense of defeat, I was thankful for the opportunity to earn a regular wage, however small it might be. While not prestigious, it was something, a start.

Working at the Strand was a perfect "recovery" job. It wasn't overly stressful or challenging, and consistent employment was practically guaranteed. Many artists, writers, and musicians worked there, and quite a few were in the program. The job at the Strand allowed me to attend meetings regularly, and I made several lifelong friends. In a very real sense I learned how to be a friend all over again, to say nothing of the benefits of showing up and being true to one's word. When I received my first pay envelope, which contained $95 in cash, I was both happy and proud.

Increasingly concerned, I alerted Lisa's family about her drinking. Everyone repeatedly stressed her need to get help, but she steadfastly refused. At last I felt I had no choice but to tell her that I would need to file for divorce unless she relented.

"You can't divorce me," she said. "I want to divorce you."

When I outlined the available choices, she opted to sue me for "abandonment."

Because we had no children or shared property, it was done without much ceremony. The separation was all too easy, sadly so. Our marriage, when it was over, had been inconsequential, empty. I don't believe we ever loved each other, not beyond raising a glass or clinging to one another for reassurance and occasional solace. We were great drinking buddies and little else. Alcohol had brought us together and, in the end, forced us to go our separate ways. When we parted it was almost as if the marriage had never happened, and that has always struck me as a small tragedy.

For the next two years mine was a relatively simple life. I bunked for short periods with various friends, subletting small apartments when they became available. Continuing to work at the Strand, I did some freelance editing and stayed close to people in recovery. The relative absence of emotional upheaval was most welcome, and my reduced circumstances seemed a small price to pay for peace of mind.

In the Spirit of Crazy Horse, my father's extensive overview of the oppression suffered by Native American peoples, was published in 1983. At its center is the story of Leonard Peltier, the American Indian Movement (AIM) member serving a life sentence for the murder of two FBI agents at Wounded Knee in 1973. Lawsuits were triggered by allegations of corruption and criminal misconduct by the governor of South Dakota and an FBI agent, and the book was removed from store shelves shortly after its release. My father's voice was effectively silenced while these cases made their way through the court system over the next seven years, and he was forced to devote much of his time to his defense.

More than anything else, he feared that the revelations about his former CIA involvement would compromise his relationships with Peltier and others he had supported. I still hadn't worked up the courage to confess my transgression, my guilt exacerbated by these developments and the publicity surrounding them. In the end, no permanent damage was done, and Peltier proved to be more forgiving than either "Doc" Humes or George Plimpton. But my father's past would continue to dog him, and he never fully emerged from its shadow.

At the conclusion of his study I traveled to Boston to meet with Dr. Berson. Sitting together in the same examining room where we had first met, he revealed that I had been on a low dose of vitamin A mixed with vitamin E, and that his original hypothesis had not been borne out. His cheeks were furrowed, and the beginnings of dark circles showed under his eyes. He pledged his ongoing commitment to research, and I offered myself as a subject whenever he might need one. Smiling, he promised to call if I could be of any help. Not sure I would ever see him again, I thanked him for everything he had done. We embraced, and he encouraged me not to give up hope.

Walking up 8th Avenue late one evening, I realized I couldn't see much at all. The street was often in shadow, and it was hard to distinguish anything, even movement. I stayed close to a friend from whom I was renting a room, using his voice and footsteps as markers in the darker stretches. Other than participating in Dr. Berson's research, I still hadn't done anything to prepare for a future as a blind man. Badly shaken by not being able to see on a brightly lighted street, I couldn't think of how I should direct my life. At thirty, if Dr. Berson's prognosis was accurate, I didn't have much time to plot a new course.

Nine

"THERE," HE SAID, AND GOT OUT OF THE TRUCK.

The snake was big, close to six feet. Curled on the desert hard-pan, it turned to face him, its coils tightening as the last wisps of fog dissolved into an azure blue sky. Except for the snake's liquid sidewindings, there was no sound or movement, no wind or distant birdsong. It was as if everything but the rocks and cacti had gone underground to escape the coming heat.

Inching his way forward as he crouched, my father stopped when the snake raised its tail and sounded its distinctive rattle. Now they were no more than six feet apart. Just out of striking range, I guessed. Neither he nor the snake moved, their eyes locked.

Without retreating, my father stood up. He didn't speak.

His eyes unwavering, I knew he was calculating his chances. He had caught copperheads with his hands as a boy, and had often boasted of that prowess. But he was fifty-seven now, and this was no copperhead. Watching in paralyzed silence, I realized for the first time that he was getting older. Did he still possess sufficient hand-eye coordination? Would years of Zen training have sharp-ened his concentration enough to compensate for slowed reflexes? The risk was enormous, since a bite from a snake this large might well kill him. We were far from a major road, and it would probably take several hours to reach a doctor, never mind a hospital. Given how long he stood there, he must have thought he had at least an even chance.

"Don't do it, Dad," I said. "Please." He didn't respond, and I began to feel a loss I had never imagined.

He crouched down again, and the snake's tail resumed its warning. When he leaned forward, almost imperceptibly, the snake pulled back its head and the rattling rose to a frenzy. No one moved, and they held each other with their eyes. Steel ticked in the heat beneath the truck's hood.

Commissioned by *Geo* magazine to write an article on the remote islands in the Sea of Cortez, he had invited me to come along. I recalled Baja's arid barrenness, with stark, angular mountains in the north and rolling stretches of desert farther south, and accepted at once. The prospect of returning to one of the more alluring places I had ever visited prompted me to hunt out Jonathan's photograph of an abandoned house north of San Felipe, its wooden ladder ascending past the roof and into the sky.

After landing on a remote desert airstrip, we were met by Dan Budnik, a wildlife photographer assigned to cover our journey. That night we camped among the boojum, an armless cactus endemic to the region. Reaching a height of fifteen feet before curling over on themselves, sometimes sporting a lone orange flower at their tips, they looked almost comical in their harsh environment. Only their tops were visible above an early morning fog, a scene reminiscent of science fiction or fantasy films.

Suddenly he was up, pulling himself back. "Nope," my father said, "not today." Keeping his eyes on the rattler until he was at a safe distance, he turned and rejoined us. No one spoke for several moments, and it was hard to read his downward gaze.

At last Dan said, "I'm glad you didn't try it, Peter. I'm glad you're all right." My father's muted grunt signaled that nothing more would follow.

The next morning we boarded the El Dorado, a dilapidated cabin cruiser, and headed for a small island with the familiar name of Sal Si Puedes. Translating to "escape if you can," it was obviously no paradise for humans. On the way my father pointed out different birds and a school of porpoise, but I just couldn't see them. Either they were too far away or moved too quickly across my limited field of vision. Even with his binoculars the effort was futile. When he placed a hand on my shoulder, I knew this pained him, too. I had never been sufficiently interested in birds to study them, but I longed to see the rare species of falcons and grebes which so excited him that day.

Only fifteen years earlier I had trained those same lenses on the floor of Ngurdoto Crater. As I looked down into its unspoiled wilderness, its steep walls prohibiting trespass by car, it was as if his binoculars had transported us back in time. With rhinos, antelope, grasslands, a small stand of trees, and a watering hole, Ngurdoto appeared to be East Africa in perfect miniature, forever preserved and protected. On that same trip I'd had no trouble picking out a pack of wild dogs on a distant knoll, the nostrils of a hippo otherwise covered by a swampy pond, and a cheetah running at full speed across the plain. How much of that would I be able to see now, I wondered. And in another fifteen years, ten, five? I would try my best to see everything, for both our sakes.

"There!" he shouted. "Right in front of us!"

A great tail rose high out of the water, its flukes still swimming before crashing back down. A spout misted in the warm, humid air. We had come upon a pod of seven or eight finback whales, a species common to these waters. Growing up to seventy-five feet, they were massive, magnificent against the horizon. I had never seen whales and couldn't have imagined how excited I would be. No other animal, even the elephants of Manyara, the lions of the

Serengeti, or the large sharks of the Australian reefs had awed me like this. I whooped in amazement, much to my father's delight.

Sal Si Puedes is a marine bird colony, hosting blue-footed boobies, cormorants, and many other species. Birds were everywhere, covering almost every inch of available ground and filling the sky. The air throbbed with shrieks and caws, and the pervasive stink of guano blanketed all other smells. A few cardon cacti stood as silent reminders that these islands were an extension of the Great Sonora Desert. Climbing the cliffs, one had to be careful of loose rock and the nests which seemed to occupy even the smallest niches. That night we fell asleep to the muffled sounds of the sea, with only occasional whisperings from the nesting birds above.

Before drifting off, I recalled a day ten years earlier, when I had gone out to Springs with Jonathan after learning that the house had been destroyed by fire. Staring at the fingers of black char which streaked from its broken windows as we got out of the car, I knew there would be nothing left. Only the front door had escaped the flames. The string of Indian bells still hung on its inside, smut all but obliterating the reds and yellows. Everything else was there, too, but forever transformed. The Masai spear still stood in its corner, Mike's table was still in place, and two Japanese dogs still guarded the fireplace, but everything was black, with the fragile and smudgy consistency of charcoal.

The books stood erect on their shelves, their spines now illegible. Jonathan reached out with his forefinger, and what had been a hardcover volume crumbled at his touch. All the books were lost, reduced to an ashy black from the outside in. With night coming on, they were disappearing into their own grayness, as indistinguishable as the charred walls which had once held so much abstract color. Much of what I saw that afternoon has faded from memory, but I will never lose the image of that huge tail against the sky.

The next day the El Dorado took us on to San Pedro Martir,

appearing in the distance as a huge rock mound rising out of the water. As we approached, my father insisted that I not climb the main promontory, stressing that attempting to find adequate hand- and foot-holds with my reduced vision would be foolhardy. I acquiesced, unable to dispute his logic, but bristled inside.

Anchoring off the island's only beach, we were greeted by a colony of sea lions as our dinghy neared the shore. The bull, by far the largest specimen at nearly five hundred pounds, bellowed a warning but retreated behind a rock as we drew closer. The cows seemed to bark more out of concern than aggression, and the pups, who kept silent, appeared to have no fear at all.

Like Sal Si Puedes, San Pedro Martir was home to thousands of birds. We decided to climb the formidable crag from the landward side, but quickly discovered that this route was only slightly less challenging. As my father noted in the 1984 *Geo* article:

So for Luke, sweating hard in the heat of the closed ravine and desperately searching for secure purchases in the loose rock, it is inevitably a difficult business. Knowing that it is necessary he is content that I remain alert, but hates it when I hover.

"Okay, Daddy-O," he says when I murmur a warning. "I hear you." Though he never asks for help, he is much better at accepting it now than he was only a few years ago. So far he is doing fine, yet over and over he scares me with lost foot-holds, grabs and stumbles. Whether or not he scares himself, I do not know, as he never complains.

Upon reaching the summit we were at eye level with birds floating on the updrafts from the water below. I was enchanted by the arrival of a tropic bird, which circled overhead several times, its streaming tail and bright red beak almost translucent in the sun. When we got safely back to sea level, I celebrated by taking a swim.

133

With the bull again grunting bombastic protests from behind his rock, I was soon joined by several pups. They came almost within reach, their watchful mothers just behind.

Our journey to the desert sea was the last trip I took with my father. In addition to his reflections on the region, the *Geo* article centers on my advancing blindness. He acknowledges his "unreasonable" pleasure when I joined him in marveling at the natural world, noting that it was important to him that I see these things "in case" I lost more vision. His desire to show me those wonders was a tremendous gift. As always, I was both fascinated and eager to see more, unaware that this was the last time we would travel together. When I read the article I was especially touched by that "in case." Like the rest of the family, he was well aware of Dr. Berson's prognosis, and I have no doubt that his denial of it was a reflection of love.

Before Christmas dinner, my father and I took our traditional walk to the beach. Now two years sober, I decided it was time to come clean about my drunken breach. A cold gray light smudged the contours of the fallow potato field, and a harsh wind muffled the honking of geese clustered at its far end. As we neared the ocean I noticed that ice had formed at the base of the tall reeds on the pond's shore. A few ducks were out on the water. "Teal," he said, and a gust of wind took me back almost twenty years.

We had huddled in his rowboat just after dawn, I in the bow and he in the stern, waiting for the ducks to come. I was twelve, and it was the first time I had joined him on a hunt. My hands and feet painfully numb, I hoped it would be the last. The December wind blew hard off the water, and I kept my head down.

They came in low out of the east, two birds in silhouette flying fast. I raised my gun and followed, leading the first just slightly, and fired. The gun roared, momentarily blocking out all other perception. The wind and cold returned as the blast echoed back from shore, and water rippled against the hull.

My father lay in the bottom of the boat, absolutely still. For a moment I didn't understand why he was there. As if watching a film, I began to comprehend what had happened, too numb to move or scream.

At last he stirred and started to rise. Eyes closed and teeth clenched, he held one hand to his ear. Shaking his head as he pulled himself back on to the seat, he stared at me through his grimace. I sat frozen, silent, my eyes on him.

"That was awfully close," he said at last. When he pulled his hand away, I saw no blood. I put the gun down and never went hunting again.

My confession didn't take long, and he didn't interrupt. Walking into the west wind beside a quiet sea, we bent our heads against the cold, avoiding eye contact. My voice rose as both hands fidgeted in their pockets, the wind doing nothing to muffle my words. Although I took "full responsibility," it was with the caveat that such a betrayal would never have happened had I been sober. After a long pause he said he doubted my culpability but, regardless, we would move on. As if to confirm a family penchant for unreasonable hope, I longed for him to say something more, to exonerate me with tears of loving forgiveness. They didn't come, and he never brought it up again.

I was beginning to feel a need for something more, something beyond not drinking, going to meetings, and living from hand to mouth. Renewing my campaign to get back into publishing, I discovered that the passage of time hadn't made things any easier. I was still a reader for two paperback houses, but couldn't get a full-time foot in any door. Eager for a change and higher wages, I took a job as a telemarketer for a shady police brotherhood association but quit at lunchtime on my first day and asked the Strand to take me back. Three months later I finally secured an editorial position at Jason Aronson, a small publisher of psychiatric and psychological texts, but was let go after only a few weeks when Dr.

Aronson was forced to cut staff. As before, I was welcomed back at the Strand.

It was finally dawning on me that my future didn't lie in publishing, and I had no lingering fantasies of ever becoming a writer. In his Christmas toast my father had looked at Rue, now living and working in Brooklyn, Alex, in college in California, and me and said, "God forbid that any of my children should ever want to write." While there was a touch of disappointment in the humor, I interpreted his remark as a release, a signal that he didn't hold it against me for abandoning the world of letters. Still without an alternative, I was keenly aware that my time was running out.

In my fourth year of sobriety I was invited to be a guest speaker at Smithers. Passing through the heavy iron doors, I introduced myself to the nurse, a woman I didn't recognize, and assured her that I could find my way upstairs. The patients began to file in as I sat facing them, and I took special note of the man who took "my" old chair. Dark haired and skinny, he wore thick horn rims and had the hollow cheeks and pitted skin of a junkie. Like those before me, I introduced myself as a grateful recovering alcoholic, touching on how much I had resented hearing that when in their seats and what had changed since then.

On my way out I ran into Renee. "Are you still thinking about becoming a counselor?" she asked.

"You're kidding, right?" I replied. "No. I took your advice and haven't given it a second thought."

"Well, that was then and this is now," she said. "I think you should consider getting into the field. You'd be good at it, and I'd be happy to write you a letter of recommendation."

She explained that the Hazelden Foundation offered a year-long counselor training program and gave me their address. With nothing to lose, I sent away for an application. Initially put off by the depth of personal information requested, I wasn't at all sure I wished to open myself to that degree. But since I had no other prospects, I returned it and hoped for the best. Three weeks later I received an invitation to come to Minnesota for an interview.

On the flight out I attempted to memorize the 12 Steps and other key program concepts. Because Hazelden's approach to addiction treatment was entirely steeped in that model, I knew I needed to sound like a true disciple if I hoped to gain entry into that hallowed recovery Mecca. The man next to me was belting back double scotches as fast as he could, and eyed me suspiciously when he saw what I was reading. Boarding the van two hours later, I nodded to my companion from the plane, who stared back with even more distrust.

By November, winter had already come to the prairie. Snow covered the rolling hills as we made our way north, the deeper declivities marking the many frozen lakes. When the driver announced that we had arrived at Center City, home to Hazelden, I saw lakes on either side of the road and no more than three or four scattered buildings. There was no sign of a city, and I didn't see how this could be the center of anything. Located just outside town, Hazelden appeared at first glance to be larger than the town itself.

On the way back to the airport I was sure I'd never see Center City again. A staff psychologist had administered the Minnesota Multiphasic Personality Inventory (MMPI), a screening which would yield a highly accurate and detailed profile. Once they got a look at the real me, what lay beneath the surface, I was sure that all hope would be lost. I was also convinced that I had seemed disingenuous and awkward, unsure of myself, in both the individual and group interviews, and was considering my next move to find another career before the plane left the tarmac.

Some months earlier a friend had introduced me to Jean, a tall, striking woman with long black hair and the olive skin common to those whose ancestors hailed from southern Italy. She was a figurative painter with a master's degree from Pratt, and her small apartment doubled as her studio. Intriguing and independent, she was funny but prone to bursts of intense anger. While we didn't exactly fall into each other's arms, we grew steadily closer. Finally, in spite of some mutual wariness, I moved out of my last illegal sublet and into her perpetually dark rooms.

Three months after my interview I received a letter which began: "As you know, you have been accepted to the chemical dependency Counselor Training Program at the Hazelden Foundation." This was news to me, and I was due to arrive in just a few weeks. Since I would be away for a year, there was a lot to tie up, and the future of my relationship with Jean was uncertain at best.

"I'm not going to sit here pining away for you," she said one night. While this struck me as a bit harsh, I got the point.

I spent the first six months of my time at Hazelden lodged in an old fisherman's motel on the shore of South Center Lake. Looking out the window after settling in, I smiled at the irony of that moment, recalling all I'd done to avoid coming here while in Smithers. At sunset, with the temperature hovering near zero, the vermilions and yellows of the huge sky cast a faint glow over the snow-covered lake. The firmament seemed to ascend forever, as if the entire universe lay atop the land. Even the big skies of Australia couldn't rival this, didn't have the same sense of limitless dimension.

Also in my view was a rusted car wreck, which rested on the lake about twenty yards from shore. Someone explained that the local saloon hauled it out every year, and its patrons took bets on the exact date it would fall through. Ice fishing was also a popular winter pastime, and there were always several huts on the lake. Inside, the sportsmen were said to have all the comforts of home, including television and plenty of liquor.

Just about everyone in Minnesota was Scandinavian, with Swedes and Norwegians in the majority. Native Americans, mostly Ojibwe, made up a much smaller percentage of the population. One of these, Jan Connors, was my classmate. She had a round, warm face, with copper skin and eyes which hinted at her Asian roots. Discovering that she knew Leonard Peltier, we soon became close friends. Like everyone else in our class of eight, Jan had come to training in search of a more rewarding vocation, hoping to establish a career which might benefit her people. One weekend we went to see *The Mission*, a beautifully filmed depiction of the brutality perpetrated on the Guarani Indians by Portuguese slave traders in eighteenth-century Brazil. At the end of a particularly brutal scene I sensed she was crying and asked whether she wanted to leave.

"No," she replied. "I need to see this."

Training at the "Great Brick Mother," as Hazelden was fondly referred to, was a combination of lectures and hands-on experience. I was assigned a small caseload on a men's unit and, from the outset, learned some of the most important lessons from my mistakes. Phil Kavanaugh, my first supervisor, was tall and lanky and sported a full red beard. He had entered treatment the day after graduating from law school and had never practiced as an attorney. Inspecting the certificates which adorned his wall, I noticed that his law degree hung upside down.

"Luke," he said at the end of my first quarter, "my goal for you is that someday you'll allow yourself to be the same person on the outside as you are on the inside." I had never considered that just being myself might be good enough, and silencing the lingering echoes of self-denunciation would prove to be both the biggest challenge and greatest reward of my recovery.

The "camel" ceremony never failed to inspire. On the night before someone's departure a small pin in the shape of a camel was passed from man to man. With "24" stamped on its side, the camel symbolized everyone's ability to stay away from a drink for one day. Holding the pin, each spoke of his connection to the departing peer, wished him well, and said goodbye. After receiving his camel, the graduate closed out the ceremony by bidding farewell to the others. One night an elderly Episcopalian minister, making no effort to hide his tears, finished by saying, "I've been in the God business for a long time, but I didn't know the first thing about spirituality until I came here."

Jean and I met monthly, alternating the travel. Maybe she wasn't pining away, but we had fallen in love. After Jan and I picked her up at the airport one Friday evening, I popped the question. My proposal came out lightly, with a playful nonchalance, in case she thought me mad or ridiculous. I don't believe either of us would have been comfortable in a more traditional setting, with me on one knee and a Hallmark vista in the background, and maybe the quirkiness of that moment made it easier, relieved some of the tension. "Sure," she replied with a big smile, and we stopped at a shopping mall to purchase wedding bands. Since we wanted to pull it off before she returned to New York, I asked a Lutheran minister in pastoral training to tie the knot, and we secured a license at the Center City Courthouse.

Jean and I were wed that Sunday beneath spectacular cliffs on the St. Croix River. Only a few friends from Hazelden were in attendance, and neither family was notified beforehand. Following a wedding night in a local motel, marred only by a broken air conditioner, Jean flew home. A few weeks later she called to ask that I arrange to be in New York on September 7th. Her reckoning turned out to be flawless, and our first child was expected in early summer.

After six months on a men's unit I transferred to extended care, which was set apart from the main complex and catered to chronic relapsers. Sister Marie, one of the counselors, often referred to herself as "the junkie nun," a reference to her past addiction to pain medication. Upon learning that I was to be a father, she decided that I needed to quit smoking.

"Luke, do you want to leave Jean a widow? Are you going to leave her all alone, with no one to help her raise that poor child?"

She was relentless, and I finally began to abuse Nicorette gum to ease my guilt and keep her at bay.

During a meeting with Russell Forrest, the unit supervisor, I learned that a famous rock star was transferring from primary care. Originally from New York, Russell was short, topped by a full head of unruly black hair, and usually had a plastic straw sticking out of his mouth. "I'd love to work with him," I said.

"No, I think I'm going to give him to Sister Marie," he replied, a mischievous grin playing across his features.

"You can't do that, Russell. You just can't," I pleaded.

In staff meeting that afternoon he said, "Marie, there's a John __ coming over tomorrow, and I'd like you to work with him."

"All right, Russell," she replied in her soft Texas drawl. "What can you tell me about him?"

"He's a musician. Why don't you stop in a record store on your way home and look at some __ albums."

"All right," she replied, quiet and unsuspecting.

The next morning she flew into his office. "Russell, I can't work with that man. He eats chicken heads and desecrates the Cross. I cannot and will not work with that man."

"Calm down, Marie," Russell replied. "You need to give him a chance, get to know him. He has the disease of addiction, just like anyone else."

He came over that afternoon in a three-piece suit, his hair cropped and wearing enough cologne to fell a skunk. A few days later Sister Marie declared, "Now don't you say anything bad about my John. All those things you heard about him, they made him do it. It was all just for publicity. That's not the real John." Enfolding him in her wings, she was like an angelic mother hen.

Assigned to a women's unit in my last quarter, my first client was Shirley, a soft-spoken Southerner in her mid-thirties. Shirley had been raped by her uncle and husband, both of whom were born-again preachers. Addicted to alcohol and Valium, she was severely depressed and remained on suicide watch for most of her treatment. She blurted out her entire story in our first session, and seemed to trust me within minutes. I was anxious and on guard, acutely aware of the pitfalls this situation presented—how vulnerable she was, how much she had been hurt by a misplaced trust in men, and her lack of boundaries. Because I needed her to believe that her life would get better, I was doing most of the talking by the time we wrapped up.

Elsa Sorensen, my new supervisor, asked how I was faring the next day. An older woman, Elsa was motherly and elegant in both manner and dress. Proud of how I had handled Shirley's outburst, I listed the interventions I had made, certain of her approval.

When I finished, she sighed and said, "You did what all men do with women. Men either try to 'fix' us, or placate us. What you need to understand is that we just want to be listened to. Not fixed, not made more comfortable, just listened to, heard. Nothing more."

It was an invaluable lesson, one which I would later appreciate didn't apply solely to women. Shirley's husband came for family treatment just before she left, and we met for a joint session. Relaxed and confident, she assured him that, if he ever forced himself on her again, she would have him arrested. She spoke calmly and with love, but there was no mistaking the sincerity of her words.

I wonder today whether I would have gone to Minnesota had I been able to find a place in publishing. Still not fully accepting that blindness should dictate my next career choice, I had seen the probability that counseling didn't require sight as little more than a propitious coincidence. On one level my year at Hazelden began as a suspension of time, another reprieve from having to face my future as a blind man. As if to facilitate further evasion, I was driven everywhere and never had to negotiate dark or crowded streets. Even the voluminous documentation was dictated into small recorders, appearing neatly typed in the chart the next morning, so I didn't need to write and could still read well enough to get by.

What I couldn't have known prior to my arrival was that I had at last found my passion and life's work. To help another person restore the foundations of dignity and purpose, to witness the flickering return of hope and joy to one who, like me, had given up on happiness, was extraordinarily gratifying. For the first time, I experienced the rewards of serving others, a spiritual gift far beyond any I had previously imagined. By year's end, I had made important strides toward realizing Phil Kavanaugh's goal of self-acceptance, a shift which would have profound implications for how I saw myself in the world, both personally and professionally. That eyesight wasn't required was still of secondary importance, but now for a very different reason.

Smithers offered me a job shortly before my graduation. I had hoped to return to the mansion, to work with Renee and Bob, but there were no openings and I began my new career at the outpatient center. Standing alone in the dusty quiet of the medical records room one afternoon, I came upon my own chart. My pulse quickened as I took it out of the rack, a sure sign that it would've been wiser to let it slide back, but curiosity won out. The first thing I saw was a Polaroid taken on the day I was admitted in 1982. Bloated and pale, I looked lost, beaten down, and at least fifteen years older than my actual age. When I read some of the notes, in which I was frequently quoted, I regretted having given in to temptation. To see how sick I had been, while enlightening in one sense, was also deeply disturbing.

As my mother drove me to the East Hampton train station not long after my return from Minnesota, I estimated that I now had no more than a thirty-five-degree visual field. In order to see the side of the road, anything that wasn't directly in front of the car, I was forced to shift my gaze. In the city I bumped into people regularly, which sometimes prompted heated exchanges, and was reluctant to go out in the evening. While completely open with Jean about my prognosis, at thirty-four I still held out a secret hope that my vision might stabilize. She would later claim she had been "duped," but I suspect that, like me, she had avoided taking a hard look at the reality of my impending blindness until I came home.

Christopher was born on June 3, 1987. He was a beautiful boy, and I dubbed him "Baby man." Grateful that I could still see him, I was enormously relieved that he was free of RP, and I would never have to suffer the guilt experienced by my mother. From his first days I took careful note of him, as if composing photographs for the album of memory.

My relationships with many of my friends and family changed dramatically after I got sober, and Christopher's arrival initiated another shift. Jonathan had never forgiven me for getting married and was increasingly discomfited by my vision loss. After I became a father, we both understood that the old days were gone for good. Since I was back in the West Village I saw Jackie regularly, but we no longer went barhopping or fished until dawn, and ultimately couldn't sustain our former closeness.

My mother turned sixty a few months after Christopher's birth, and neither reaching that milestone nor becoming a grandmother sat particularly well with her. If not exactly a coffin nail, he was irrefutable proof that she was getting older, perhaps the worst fear of a woman who hoped to die "thin, with all my marbles, and a good tan." She drew nearer after he learned to talk, but was never fully relaxed in his infant presence.

My father was glad that one of his progeny had finally produced a grandchild. Like my mother, he didn't show much interest until Christopher grew into a little person, leaving most of the early grandparenting to Maria.

Mike was more or less indifferent to my becoming a father, and never saw himself in the role of grandfather. The change in our relationship revolved around alcohol. Along with my mother, he was wary of my sobriety and new profession. I never preached to either of them about their drinking, since I couldn't imagine anything more odious than a proselytizing teetotaler, but Mike seemed worried that I might judge him.

"I stopped drinking martinis, and I thought you'd like to know," he said a few months after my return from Minnesota.

"That's good, Mike," I replied.

"Yes, but I still drink wine," he said.

Unable to stop myself, I asked, "How much?"

"About two bottles a day, but it's very good wine."

Jean and I adored our child, but we didn't have an easy time of it. The only spot for the crib was a narrow space between a bookcase and a shelf which held her stereo equipment. We had little money and were forced to roll coins more than once to buy good coffee or have the laundry done, two luxuries we refused to give up.

On weekends we often took Christopher to a nearby park. Of all the images I remember from his first year, a photograph taken there stands out. Laying on a swing, he is dressed in a New York Yankees cap and jacket, and staring straight into Jean's camera. His look is one of grim determination, but there is a suggestion of an incipient wink. I still recall that expression whenever I catch myself taking things just a little too seriously.

Although Jean and I loved one another, the seeds of discontent were sown in fertile ground. I worked full-time, including two nights, so she had to devote most of her day to the baby. When I subsequently enrolled in a part-time graduate program in social work, I had even less time for my family. Without a master's degree, I knew there was no hope for future advancement and higher wages. Jean refused to give up painting, and my schedule became a source of regular friction. While I stressed the need to ready ourselves for the days ahead, she insisted on retaining her identity as an artist. We couldn't afford childcare of any sort and began to argue more frequently. Underneath everything else, like a toxic chemical seeping into the groundwater, our separate fears about my blindness fueled the discord as we struggled to find a compatible balance. When she announced her desire to have another child, I couldn't have been more surprised.

Ten

T HEY FACED ONE ANOTHER, THEIR BODIES CURLED SLIGHTLY inward. With heads bowed, they might have been playing chess in a distant galaxy, light years away. We looked at them as if through a telescope, the image drifting in and out of focus on unseen currents. They were a portrait of tranquility, unconcerned and undisturbed, unaware of our intrusion into their private world.

"I thought so," I said, unable to suppress a nervous laugh.

"Oh, my God," Jean said, the picture on the screen slipping away with the movement of her body.

"Do you want to know the sex?" the technician asked, adjusting his scanner to get a better look.

"Why not," she replied. "I don't think I'm up for any more surprises."

"Boys," he said. Watching as the picture settled back into focus, I marveled at his ability to read the image so precisely. While we had no trouble discerning two distinct figures, the black-and-white sonogram at first glance looked more abstract than photographic, requiring some concentration to distinguish form and depth. Because they were in a sitting position, their legs tucked slightly up, I didn't see how he had determined the gender.

"Since we have dispensed with surprises," the technician continued, "I should also tell you that they are identical."

"Oh, my God," Jean repeated, the twins again sliding out of view as she laughed.

"How do you know?" I asked.

"The same umbilical sac," he replied. "Fraternals would be in separate sacs because there are two eggs. With identicals the egg splits, so there's only one sac."

"Incredible," I murmured. For my part, I could see no sac at all.

"You're not shocked?" Jean asked. "You don't seem surprised."

"I'm not, really," I replied with a cough. "Stunned, yes, but not surprised. I didn't tell you I thought it was twins because I didn't want you to worry. You're just so much bigger than last time."

"Jesus, we have to move," she observed.

"That's for sure," I said.

Only a faint gray light ever found its way to our windows, but it was enough to confirm that we couldn't possibly wedge in another crib, never mind two. Sitting together on the sofa, trying not to panic, we attempted to reassure one another that we would find a way to manage. With the prospect of caring for three children under two, our future was certain to be radically different from anything we had planned. In a perpetual state of flux since Christopher's birth, we had been preparing for a stability which we now knew would continue to elude us. To that end Jean had secured a part-time position as a graphic designer at *Newsweek*, and I had left Smithers for a better paying job with Larry Barnett, whom I had met in Minnesota. Larry was the first drug addict ever treated at Hazelden, and now had his own aftercare business near Columbus Circle. Portly and mustachioed, he looked like an Irish police detective. Originally a tough kid from Queens and a former Marine, he was good-natured and impish, and always treated me more like a partner than an employee.

Our neighbor came in with Christopher, assuring us that he had been delightful company, no trouble at all. Taking him in her arms, Jean walked several times around the kitchen, kissing him repeatedly before placing him back in his crib. He was a joy for both of us, but from the first it was clear he was Jean's child. As much as she sometimes had difficulty coping with the demands of an infant, she bestowed a special love on him, not unlike my mother's for me. Theirs was a closeness reserved only for each other.

Neither jealous nor resentful, I had been hoping for a daughter this time around, one who would be mine. She was to be called Regina, with Delregno, my mother-in-law's maiden name, to follow. But when I learned that male twins were on the way, I whispered a silent farewell to my unborn queen.

Since a larger place in Manhattan was beyond our means, we set our sights on Brooklyn. A brief search turned up a three-bedroom apartment above a dry cleaner in Bay Ridge, on a main thoroughfare and close to the subway. Its rooms were boxlike and without much character, but the added space and cheaper rent were well worth the long commute on the R train. We didn't know it then, but we had left Manhattan for good.

Several weeks before the twins were due, Piedy came out with a crib that had been used by her grandchildren. The beach picnics had ended decades earlier, and she and Peter Gimbel had been divorced for years. She was now married to Sydney Lumet, and I usually saw her only on Christmas Eve at my father's house. Pulling up in her Mercedes station wagon, Piedy looked grand indeed, especially in our neighborhood.

"Hello, Lucas," she said as she got out of the car. "I hear you've got some babies coming." With the same humor and thoughtful kindness I remembered as a young boy, she helped us haul the crib upstairs.

Mike now spent half the year in Italy, but I visited his studio whenever I could. It was becoming more difficult to see his paintings, to appreciate the nuances of light and color, but I did my best not to dwell on it.

"You know," he said as we split a huge corned beef sandwich one afternoon, "I've just sold four paintings to the Sheikh of Yemen. Big ones, and he paid top dollar for them. He's flying me over in his private jet for the installation and, of course, I'll be staying at the palace."

Pausing, I asked, "That's great, Mike, but why would the Sheikh of Yemen buy four paintings from a guy named Goldberg?"

With no trace of embarrassment or awkwardness, he smiled and replied,

"I told him my name was O'Goldberg."

I loved him as much as ever and, as with Piedy, treasured the continuity of his periodic presence in my adult life.

Larry and I quickly became close friends. Always open and giving, he was genuinely interested in me and my family. We spent hours exchanging anecdotes which highlighted the many differences in our backgrounds and experience, all the reasons we should never have been so compatible. Alcoholism ran like a freight train through both sides of his family, but he inevitably separated the person from their drinking. As horrific as some of his stories were, Larry never recounted them with bitterness, hurt, or resentment, but rather with humor and love.

More than anyone previously, including therapists and sponsors, Larry made it safe to look beneath the rosy veneer I had painted over much of my past. While my first instinct was still to remember only the good times and how well I was treated, Larry helped me acknowledge the less-romantic side of everyone's drinking without feeling like I was somehow betraying them. The discussions in his smoke-filled office, always buoyed by a lot of laughter, allowed me to see the many dimensions of those who had peopled my childhood, to develop a kind of "second sight" into my past. Neither gods nor demons, they were complicated, brilliant, loving, occasionally selfish, wonderful, and flawed human beings. Larry helped me in ways no one ever had, and his gift, when I managed to hold on to it, was tremendously liberating.

"I've got a problem," one of my clients said at the opening of his first session. Two of Jean's paintings hung in my office, a still life and a portrait of a friend whose expression mirrored how I must have looked when confronted in group seven years earlier.

"What's your problem?" I asked.

"My uncle is the vice president, my girlfriend works for the Dukakis campaign, and I voted for Jesse Jackson."

"You've got a problem," I confirmed. Later we got around to the issue of his prescription drug abuse.

Another introduced himself by saying, "I'm a little late."

"Really?" I asked, stealing a quick look at my watch. "What time was your appointment?"

"Three years ago," he replied.

My work with these men, many of whom were stockbrokers, investment bankers, and corporate managers, was an important part of my spiritual and professional growth. Witnessing the healing which began when they revealed their fears and insecurities, their compassion and humanity, always reinforced the reasons I had chosen my field. These were men for whom I wouldn't have thought it possible to feel much empathy, but they helped me face the biases which otherwise would have limited my ability to work with them, and I was richly rewarded for having done so.

The twins were due in early April of 1989, and by mid-March the physics of how Jean remained upright were hard to fathom. On the 23rd, the day before my birthday, she went into Manhattan to get me a present and visit her friends at *Newsweek*. That night, at about 1 a.m., she woke me and said, "Happy birthday." Initially bewildered, I finally realized what was happening and called a cab to take us to the hospital. They were born shortly after sunrise, weighing in at over seven pounds each.

"They look like little Guidos!" Jean cried when the twins were placed in her arms. I had wanted to name them Vinnie and Sal, but she would have none of it. At last she conceded to Joseph, after her deceased father, but that was as close to Italian as she would get. We finally settled on Joseph Hale and Andrew Wright, their middle names, like Christopher's "Carey," harkening back to my ancestry.

For the next two years we got by on little sleep, since the twins were never on the same schedule. When not at work or school we did chores and took care of the children. Jean had no time to paint and never pardoned me for not fully understanding how great a sacrifice this was. While sympathetic, I was too busy to do much about it. Always worried that we wouldn't have enough to get by, I didn't then appreciate the degree to which Jean's art was truly her vocation, or how excruciating it must have been to feel like she had to choose between her art and her children.

My social work field instructor lived on 11th Street, only three blocks from where I had grown up. After the clocks were turned back in the fall of 1989, it was dark when I left her office. Heading south on West 4th Street, I couldn't see anything but the brightest lights. Although I had walked this route hundreds of times, I tripped over tree guards, bumped into passersby, and stumbled on curbs. That I had effectively lost all night vision was suddenly undeniable, and I was badly shaken. Moving slowly and standing still when footsteps approached, I finally made it to the subway entrance and the salvation of the light below.

Jean asked what was wrong as soon as I walked in. Hearing what had happened and how frightened I was, she declared, "I'm not going to be responsible for your vision any longer. You need to do something about it." Shocked by her reaction, I felt doubly wounded. How could she be so harsh, so uncaring? Didn't she realize how hard this was for me? Didn't she have a heart?

Brimming with self-pity, I pondered my situation. Her delivery didn't rate too high on the sympathy scale, but I gave no thought to how years of fear and sadness might have fueled her response. In any case, she wasn't wrong. I couldn't ask her to shoulder the burden of my blindness, especially as she now had three young boys to look after. Remembering that she had a doctor's appointment the next day and that his office was across the street from the Lighthouse, an agency serving the blind, I asked her to pick up a white cane. She gave this some thought before responding, doubtlessly weighing the benefits of acquiescing against allowing me to shirk my responsibility yet again, and reluctantly agreed.

A folded cane lay on the desk when I returned home the next day, but I passed it by with hardly a glance. In spite of recent experience and all I had learned, the cane still represented the end of almost everything joyous and meaningful in my life. Opening it would condemn me to being irreversibly inferior, and nothing could compensate for that. While I might have counseled others to look at objective reality as a means of challenging the corrosive effects of stigma, I couldn't do the same for myself.

The next night, after I bumped into him, a man asked, "What are you, fucking blind?" Fighting back an urge to rip out his throat, I apologized and continued home. Larry would later note that people generally don't make changes in their lives because it might be a good idea to do so. Instead, change usually occurs only when the risk of trying something new is finally outweighed by the pain of continued resistance. Still ignorant of this and because denial rarely gives way to rationality, I left the cane at home in the morning. But after another hair-raising commute I finally put it in my briefcase.

That night, unfolding it as I emerged from the school library, I began tapping my way toward the subway. I'd had no training and would later learn that the cane was several inches too short. It seemed to get caught in every crack and repeatedly jabbed me in the chest, but a remarkable transformation occurred almost instantly. For the first time in years I wasn't afraid as I walked in the dark.

I began to relax, no longer tensing when someone approached. Because the cane was also a signal to others, people moved aside and said "Excuse me" instead of "Asshole" or "What the fuck's the matter with you?" Quickening my step, I tapped with growing confidence and reached the subway without incident.

Several weeks later a mobility trainer came out to Brooklyn. After determining the correct length she showed me the proper way to hold and move the cane. The most important thing was maintaining a rhythm and tapping only when the foot on the opposite side was fully forward. This ensured fluidity of movement and that the cane would always hit something before I did. In addition to alerting me to objects or changes in the path ahead, I began to appreciate that the cane could almost serve as an extension of my foot or finger, that a great deal could be determined simply by paying attention to its "touch."

Jean wasn't standing on the sidelines cheering me on. Still certain that I had somehow deceived her, she felt unfairly tied to a blind man, trapped by the circumstances of motherhood and my worsening eyesight. She feared that her life as an artist was over, that she would be forever relegated to the role of the caretaker, and deeply resented me for it. In many ways, of course, she was right. As time went on I could do less and less without her assistance. My progressive inability to fulfill routine chores fueled a desire to compensate in whatever way I could, usually by vacuuming and mopping the floors. But my efforts were often unappreciated or dismissed as inadequate, and this angered me greatly.

Christopher started nursery school when he was four. Since Jean worked late on Friday nights, I picked him up on my way home. We always walked to the local diner hand in hand, singing what we came to call the "Critter song":

Because he's coming across the sea,
Just to be with you and me.

He's the little Critter man,
He's doing all he can.
He's the little Critter Pie,
He's the apple of my eye.
He's the little Christopher,
Fun for me and fun for her.

Christopher always insisted on adding a declarative "That's right!" as we pumped our hands to punctuate the song's ending. Reaching the diner, we both mooned over a beautiful black-haired Irish waitress with a bewitching brogue. When she pretended to flirt with him, Christopher smiled broadly and began to stammer, but managed to order exactly the same thing in exactly the same sequence every week. "I'll have a hamburger, French fries, salad, pickle, coleslaw, and a Coke to drink, please." The waitress repeated it back, and we all laughed. This was our special night, and I cherished it.

Christmas Eve in Sagaponack was especially festive in 1991. *Killing Mr. Watson,* the first in a trilogy of novels centered on the life of a Florida planter at the turn of the century, had been published to much critical acclaim. After years of court wrangling, my father had at last been vindicated, and *In the Spirit of Crazy Horse* was reissued to considerable fanfare. I resumed my Santa routine, now for my own children, complete with sleigh bells and the big red barrel. Piedy, who had always known what would please a child, what was special to them, arrived with three inexpensive flashlights, and my kids dropped their other Christmas booty at once.

In May we traveled to Fishers Island to celebrate my grandfather's ninetieth birthday. Once again clad in his Greek sailor's cap, my father took Christopher and me by boat to see the old house. Before we departed, Jean took a picture of us with my grandfather, four generations of Matthiessens in front of the dock where he had always kept his boats.

Lying off the small beach, we stared at the house. I could still make it out, the white balustrade of my grandmother's bedroom porch in bright contrast to the darker background. The current owners had mowed the grass in front, which my grandparents had always let grow wild, and I disapproved with proprietary righteousness. When I voiced as much to my father he initially said nothing, continuing to look toward the land. At last he said it was good that we were all together, and put his arm around Christopher and me.

We moved into a two-story apartment around the corner before the start of the school year. It had a backyard and much more room to stretch out, and Jean even set up a small studio. I was using the cane regularly, gaining both confidence and skill, and the children seemed to be happy in their new home. Larry and I had worked hard to expand the business, and I began to supervise the two clinicians he hired to meet the demand. With less stress and more time to ourselves after my graduation, Jean and I weren't fighting as often or with such intensity.

My worsening vision was now an established part of our family life, and the boys adjusted well to it. Cane in hand, I took them grocery shopping on Saturday mornings, and they quickly memorized the location of almost everything. Like a blind pasha, I stood at the head of the store and directed them as they flew through the aisles. They also helped me cook, since I couldn't always make out the height of the flame.

As I turned on to our street one afternoon, Christopher, Andy, and Joe ran out from our gate. I could see them clearly in the sharp winter light, and each held a stick. All three were laughing and I was struck by how, in different ways, our genes had combined to create such handsome children. Walking toward me, they tapped their makeshift canes from side to side, and I tapped mine in loud response. They thought this was great fun, and I delighted in their show. Converging in the middle of the block, we tapped our way home. That night I recited *Goodnight Moon* or *Harold and the Purple*

Crayon as they crowded around, turning the pages from memory in the near darkness of their bedroom.

Reading now required very bright light, and I could only see one or two words at a time. The jostling and fluorescent lighting of the subway made it extremely difficult, but I always brought something to read. It took several weeks to finish Garcia Marquez's *The General in His Labyrinth*, and I thought it might well be my last book. That I would soon be unable to read was almost unthinkable. I couldn't imagine what would take its place, what could possibly give me the same stimulation and pleasure.

While I wasn't always grateful, my vision had already lasted longer than Dr. Berson had predicted. At nearly forty, I could still see my children and discern varying levels of light, though perhaps not everything it illuminated. Doing all I could to hold on to any semblance of sight for as long as possible, I had two cataract surgeries despite being warned that this probably wouldn't make an appreciable difference. What little I could see was slightly sharper for a few months, but as my visual field continued to shrink I began to live more of life from memory.

Recalling images from my past—faces, houses, photographs, artwork, and landscapes—I concentrated on the details of each in an effort to preserve them. With hearing fast succeeding sight as my primary sense, I logged visual memories during quiet times, almost as a kind of meditation. In this way I began to build a visual library, a collection of references upon which I might frame a way to see in the dark.

The last book I read with my eyes, in 1992, was *Killing Mr. Watson*. With the exception of some of the fiction, *Blue Meridian* and *The Snow Leopard*, I had resisted reading many of my father's books. Rationalizing that I wasn't interested in the subject matter, reading his work had sometimes brought him too close and always resurrected a deep-seated suspicion that I had disappointed him. At that time I was also stewing about a recent *Vanity Fair* profile in which he noted that his divorce from my mother had "freed" him and advised that one should never call home when away "because it always ruins the trip." Now certain I would never be able to read another, I put aside my disquiet. With the book held close, I read slowly, carefully, trying not to lose my place as the train jolted and swayed.

He had first heard about Edgar Watson at age seventeen from my grandfather. Passing the mouth of the Chatham River, the site of Watson's homestead in Florida's Ten Thousand Islands, my grandfather told him of how Watson had been gunned down by his neighbors because they believed him to be guilty of multiple murders. The story had stayed with him, and his recounting of the few known facts had intrigued me long before the book was published.

From its opening pages I knew this was something extraordinary. Following a description of a pioneer settlement in the aftermath of a hurricane—mud-filled cisterns, the stench of rotting chickens, broken trees, and a dog barking "without heart"—the sound of a far-off outboard motor is heard, instantly transforming the atmosphere of exhausted devastation into one of visceral foreboding. Watson was coming.

Astounded by his ear for dialogue and the descriptive acuity of his prose, I thought the book a masterpiece. No longer just hearing about Peter Matthiessen's greatness, I had seen it for myself. To my mind he had achieved one of the highest goals imaginable, unattainable by all but the most gifted, and I was immensely proud of him.

Only later did it occur to me that charting an independent course had freed me from decades of defensive comparison. Precisely because I was so passionate about my work as a therapist, a field about which my father understood very little, it was no longer a threat to acknowledge his talent. Letting go of the gods I had created, whether Frank's Dionysus or my father's Apollo, had been the key. I had always assumed that I needed to worship both, or choose one over the other, not realizing until I went to Hazelden that my path lay with neither.

With almost no vision remaining, I knew it wouldn't be long before I couldn't see anything. It had been nearly twenty years since Dr. Berson's diagnosis, and a curious but familiar paradox had started to unfold. The more vision I lost, the less anxious I became. As with my drinking, the secret to victory was in admitting defeat. While I certainly didn't look forward to being completely blind, I was no longer convinced that my life would be over when the screen went blank. Time had smoothed over some of my initial dread at that prospect, as had the consistent support of my family. But most of all, it was the many talks with Larry which helped me to experience, however fleetingly, the serenity that Renee had promised would come with acceptance.

Eleven

Jackie returned to St. Vincent's Hospital for the third time in the fall of 1992, but few held out any hope that he might leave again. As with his sexual identity years earlier, he had attempted to hide the diagnosis, but only some members of his family had chosen not to see the truth, either then or now. Because he had not gotten sick for nearly ten years after the AIDS outbreak, I thought he might have magically escaped this fate despite countless drunken nights in the back rooms of West Village gay bars. But when Mel told me that he was suffering from an unspecified "infection," the details of which weren't forthcoming, I didn't need to ask more questions.

As I entered his room, the sounds of muted laughter rose and fell with whoops and cheers, trilling flutes, and soaring strings. A woman's voice rang out, high and strident, exhorting a crowd of children. At last they came together in a chorus of song, tinny and saccharine, the unmistakable strains of a Broadway musical. Eager for relief of any kind, I listened more carefully and realized that the tune was from *Peter Pan*. Despite its grotesque incongruity, even this was a welcome distraction.

Above his head, Christ's face was pale and emaciated, contorted in agony, with no sign of resignation or assurance of eternal glory. The Savior's eyes glared like those of a terrified cow at the cassette player, hidden behind a partially drawn curtain, and thick blood flowed from all points of the stigmata. Impaled on a large cross, the beams wider than usual, his body appeared diminished, less important than the symbol which held it.

"Goddamned HIV," Mel whispered, sobbing as he gripped his lover's hand.

Standing at the foot of the bed, I looked back down at Jackie, his thick black hair strewn on the white pillow. He slept fitfully, his breathing coming in stertorous bursts. Muttering incoherently, as if dreaming, he seemed restless, worried. His hand twitched in Mel's.

"I won't grow up, won't grow up, won't grow up, not me!"

Clutching her oversized rosary like a set of brass knuckles, Lillian Hanley, Jackie's mother and the matriarch of her clan, entered the room. Her face firm, she avoided eye contact and took her place across the bed from Mel. Although he sat no more than four feet from her, still holding Jackie's hand, she ignored him completely. She had greeted no one, and no one had dared to distract her with so much as a "hello."

Settling herself, she made the sign of the Cross. "I believe in God, the Father Almighty, Creator of Heaven and Earth . . ." Her gray head bowed, her face pockmarked and her almost toothless speech slightly slurred, she was a portrait of stolid endurance. The mother of twelve, she was on the verge of losing a second child. She had kept her family together in spite of poverty, the early death of her husband to alcoholism, and the periodic imprisonment of three sons. As the materfamilias, she had reaffirmed her dominance by the simple force of her presence. She sat with eyes closed, her features a mask of calm, her faith and authority beyond challenge.

A week earlier Mel and I had helped Jackie walk to the dayroom.

Proceeding slowly, he was unsteady and weak, his appearance almost inconceivable. The "wasting" had taken all but the core of him, and I knew he wouldn't live much longer.

"Ulie," he said, "I don't want you to see me like this."

"It's all right, Jack," I replied. "That doesn't matter now. I'm just glad to be here, and to see you walking so well." My words sounded hollow, absurd, but I couldn't think of what else to say. AIDS was taking my oldest friend, and I had no way of comforting him.

"Ulie," he repeated, just before I heard a soft splashing. Jackie began to cry. Looking down, I saw that he had defecated, the diarrhea running down his legs.

"I'll get a nurse," I said.

"I'm sorry, Ulie. I'm sorry. I didn't want you to see me like this."

"I'll clean him up," Mel said. "Please let me do it." With his thinning hair and glasses slightly askew, he looked not just fatigued, but almost broken. As I walked toward the nurse's station it occurred to me that Mel, who hadn't put on gloves, might be hoping to contract the virus.

Jackie began to stir, his brow furrowed, his mouth forming soundless words. Mel had told me that he was especially grieved about not being accepted by the Church, even when dying. Although on the AIDS ward of a Catholic hospital, he continued to feel ashamed, ultimately rejected, and unloved. Now he looked agitated and afraid. Powerless to change any of it, I flushed with angry impotence.

"I won't grow up, not a penny will I pinch, I will never grow a mustache or a fraction of an inch."

—*I believe in the Holy Ghost; the Holy Catholic Church; the communion of saints*—

"I'll never grow up, never grow up, never grow up, no sir, not I, not me, so there!"

—*the forgiveness of sins; the resurrection of the body; and the life everlasting. Amen.*

163

Jackie awoke and scanned the room. He had lost all vision several days earlier, but his eyes still moved in a reflexive imitation of sight. Following the line of Mel's arm, he glanced up to where he thought his lover's face ought to be. He muttered something, and Mel leaned in closer.

"Yes, Jack," he said. "I will always be with you."

"Hello, son," Lillian said. "I am here. Your mother is here."

Jackie shifted his gaze back and forth. Helpless and confused, he looked frantic, his eyes beseeching. Standing over him, holding my white cane like the feeblest of staffs, I could have sworn he was begging them to make peace.

"Has the priest been in today?" Lillian asked.

"Not since I've been here," I replied.

"Can someone please send for him? I'd like him to be here." Lillian's youngest child, Laurie, rose immediately, and her mother resumed her rosary.

"May I sit with him a moment, Mel?" I asked.

"Of course," he replied, hurrying out of the room.

Taking Jackie's hand, I leaned toward him and said, "I love you, Jack. I'll miss you, and thank you for everything, our friendship and all the great times we had. Try to be at peace now. Everything is all right. Goodbye, dear Jack."

Mel returned, and I gave Jackie's hand a parting squeeze. When I felt the slightest tightening of his fingers, I began to weep and resumed my place at the foot of the bed. A nurse entered and took his pulse. Jackie's breathing was labored, and he seemed to be more agitated. "It won't be long now," the nurse said quietly. "I'll see if the doctor is available."

"Our Father, who art in Heaven," Lillian began.

"My child, my very own, don't be afraid, you're not alone . . ."
"Thy kingdom come, Thy will be done . . ."
"Sleep until the dawn for all is well . . ."
The room seemed to shrink. There was only his bed and no

one else. I shut out the din of music and prayer, other voices and Mel's gentle moaning. As I watched, Jackie raised his head and again attempted to scan the room. I had never seen anyone look so frightened. His head fell back on the pillow, shook violently to the right, then back to the left, and he was gone, his tongue and eyes protruding as if he'd been choked.

The room filled with sound, but each of us remained alone in our grief. Mel wailed, Lillian prayed, the cassette player droned on, and I was speechless, my eyes locked on him. A priest entered, and I vacated my spot. He administered the last rites robotically, without love or compassion. Offering perfunctory consolation only to Lillian, he left hurriedly. Watching his retreat, I remembered that Jackie had received this sacrament once before, after he had "fallen" from a five-story roof at the age of thirteen. He was comforted then, but not this time.

* * *

Jean and I walked west on 11th Street to my old block. What had once been the corner laundry was now a high-end restaurant, the warehouse a condominium, the tenements across the street and Jackie's old building renovated into expensive apartments. Our building had been repainted a dull red, and I didn't hear any children. Continuing west to the river, I longed for a sensory reminder of my earliest days with Jackie, the soot, grit, and engine smells of the old West Side, but these had been replaced by the passing aromas of sautéed garlic and expensive perfumes. The truck bays were mostly gone, and the docks had been closed or converted into recreational areas.

Preoccupied with work, school, and taking care of the kids, I hadn't seen much of Sara Carey since moving to Brooklyn. We spoke briefly at the hospital, but rarely met in the year following Jackie's death. After promising starts in both television and publishing, she had faltered and, ultimately, withdrawn. This pattern had begun at Bennington, where she completed every requirement for graduation but her senior thesis. In more recent years, she had become progressively reclusive, pulling away from friends and shunning intimate relationships. When one day she sounded a little too sedated over the phone, I decided to pay a visit.

She lay in the dark, all but one or two bulbs burned out, and the place smelled like an unattended litter box. Her cats had ripped the upholstery of my grandmother's antique chairs, and the living room was strewn with empty food cartons. She spoke slowly, dully, her voice almost lifeless. Noticing some prescription bottles by her bed, I discovered that her psychiatrist had her on six different medications, only one of which was an antidepressant. Apart from one vitamin, the rest consisted of three tranquilizers and an amphetamine. I didn't believe she was a drug addict in the traditional sense, but guessed she was probably dependent on the benzodiazepines.

I recalled the final days of my drinking and wondered what my sister must have felt when she came to see me. Had she been any less shocked, even frightened? Sara had always claimed that her psychiatrist was brilliant, a lifesaver, but now I wondered whether hers might not be the next light to fade out. Angry at the doctor and guilty about not staying in closer touch, I promised to get help. After consulting my parents, I persuaded her to meet with Larry, and he arranged for her to go to Minnesota. She would later claim that I had orchestrated her banishment to the Midwest, but I took comfort in knowing that she was safe.

With all three children in school, life had settled down. Christopher and Joe were enrolled in a small Lutheran institution, and Andy was attending a nearby Catholic academy. Remembering the abuses she had suffered at the hands of nuns, Jean initially refused to allow any of them inside its doors. But after ruling out the local public school and agreeing that it was probably best to separate the twins, she grudgingly relented. In a photograph taken toward the end of the year, Christopher stands on a raised platform in his school blazer. He is looking up and away, his features set, his right fist clutched to his chest. With a saber strapped to his side he might have passed for a tiny Civil War general.

The RP Foundation held its 1994 conference in San Francisco, and I was invited to speak on coping with vision loss. At the end of my first workshop a young man told of how, after parking his car, he unfolded his cane to navigate sidewalks and alert others to his low vision. As crazy as the scenario sounded, I heard echoes of my own behavior and the anguish I had experienced fifteen years earlier. He joined in a smattering of sympathetic laughter before asking what I thought his next step ought to be. Trying to soften the blow of the only reasonable response, I suggested that, since he couldn't very well put a cane on the front of his car, perhaps he already had his answer.

Dr. Berson ran up and hugged me on the second day of the conference, thanking me for all I had done to help him. "One of the original pioneers," he said to anyone within earshot. He was a changed man. Humbled by his failure to find a cure, he couldn't have been more amiable. We embraced with the understanding that we had done everything we could for one another, that we had given it our best and done it together. It was wonderful to see him, to reaffirm our connection, no matter that he hadn't suc-ceeded and I was now using a white cane.

That fall Larry called me into his office and announced that he was moving back to Minnesota. Dressed in a sweatshirt and "Gophers" baseball cap, he looked uncomfortable and out of place next to his elegant wooden desk. His voice was uncharacteristi-cally subdued, and he wasn't laughing.

"Jesus, Larry. Why?" I asked. He loved New York, and the busi-ness was going well.

"I'm sorry, Luke meister," he replied. "I think it's time. I need to slow down, and this is probably too much for me right now."

Larry's wife, Nancy, had been hoping to return, but now I sensed there was something else, something he wasn't ready to disclose. He had been spending less time in the office, and looked pale and fatigued. "I'm sorry, too," I said. We had worked together for seven years. "I'll miss you, boss."

"We really had a good thing, didn't we?" he asked. "We had a lot of fun."

"We sure did," I replied. Walking back to my office, I realized I had never imagined a future without him. His accountant suggested that I stay on to run the business, but Larry was firm in his determination to shut it down. As painful as it was, I had no choice but to look for another job.

The Joseph Bulova School in Woodside, Queens, was opened shortly after World War II to provide training in watch repair to disabled veterans. Before I was hired the school had added a program in jewelry making, and now offered instruction to anyone suffering from a wide array of physical and emotional disabilities. Although I had nearly doubled my salary as the "Director of Student Affairs," I was never exactly sure what my role was. I did almost no clinical work, and rarely had the sense that my administrative oversight made an appreciable difference in the lives of the students. That uncertainty, along with a growing suspicion that the school had probably seen its day, sparked feelings of restlessness and doubt.

Larry had allowed me to see a few private clients in his office, and I requested the same privilege before accepting my new job. Given my rapid disillusionment, these periodic ties to more meaningful work were like discovering little oases on a walk across the Sahara. Freddy, another Harvard chum of Frank's, had been my client for two years and followed me out to Queens. I had first met him at the 11th Street parties, where he usually arrived with Hal Fonderin. Even more than Joe LeSueur, Freddy was renowned for his acerbic tongue and bitchy wit. When we reconnected he was in his sixties, balding, and in recovery from alcoholism. Before starting therapy he had been drawn to Buddhism, traveling to Nepal in search of spiritual growth.

After a long pause in the darkening quiet of a late afternoon session, Freddy said, "In the end, all we really have is love."

Astounded by the contrast to the man I had known long ago, I sat back and asked, "Do you think our work is done, Freddy?"

"Yes, I think it is."

Declaring that he would like us closer to Sagaponack, my father put up the down payment for a small Cape-style house on Long Island.

Jean and I had debated the pros and cons of the move for weeks, these discussions sometimes erupting into tumultuous arguments. As a painter she saw no hope for regular involvement in the art world and feared her life would soon be reduced to that of the minivan-driving soccer mom. I'd never imagined I'd be living the "suburban dream" under any circumstances, but I was torn. In the end the district's better schools, having more room to raise our kids, and the down payment we couldn't afford trumped our desire to remain in the city.

As I sat on our deck a few months later, my vision all but gone, I was treated to a fleeting image of Christopher. His hair in the shortest of ponytails, he was walking next to our yellow Labrador, Jack, under a big lime tree in the back yard. Dressed in the baggy shorts and tank top that was his perennial uniform in summer, his hand rested on Jack's back. Flickering sunlight dappled them as the breeze rustled the leaves above. By sheer luck I had looked in exactly the right spot in exactly the right light, and gasped at this momentary reminder of a sighted life. With the exception of his image in silhouette against a fountain a few weeks later, this was the last time I saw him, or anyone else, so distinctly.

Everyone appeared to be adjusting to life in the suburbs. Jean was painting in the basement, the children seemed to like their new school, and I was "reading" a great deal on my daily commute to the city. After some initial resistance I had discovered audiobooks and was now something of a patron to the local library. Determined to enrich its audio collection, which consisted primarily of self-help guides and celebrity biographies, I donated dozens of books on tape. Beginning with some of the classics—Tolstoy, Dostoyevsky, Turgenev, Dickens, Eliot, Melville, Flaubert, Hardy, Conrad, and Faulkner—I later added more contemporary writers, including Styron and Matthiessen. Supplementing the library's budget in my small way gave me a lot of pleasure, and I was always excited when new books came in.

The move to the suburbs didn't result in more frequent visits to my father. As always, he was immersed in his work. These were the "Watson" years, when he was writing the second and third novels of the original trilogy. But the kids loved to visit my mother, whom they called the "gorgeous grandma," much as Terry Southern had dubbed her "Pat Perfect" forty years earlier. After her initial reaction to Christopher's arrival, she had donned the mantle of grandmother with surprising energy and enthusiasm. She even built a room for the boys in her storage shed, with two sets of bunk beds inside, designated "the clubhouse" by a small sign out front. All three were excited by this gentle push toward independence, but they always asked me to spend the night with them. Before we drifted off I told bedtime stories over a soporific chorus of crickets, our darkened sanctuary redolent of new wood. Their favorites were the misdoings of an unfailingly stupid astronaut and their own adventures among a Pacific Islander people I named the Oomingmak. Unbeknownst to them, this was the title of one of my father's books, a short chronicle of his travels to the Arctic to see the musk ox. Christopher, in particular, delighted in these bedtime tales, and later staged many theatrical improvisations in our kitchen.

Jean first raised the idea of a guide dog in the fall of 1995. Even with the cane I was sometimes having difficulty navigating the mile-long walk from the train station, particularly after dark on the dimly lighted side streets. My decreasing vision contributed to mounting tension as I crossed large roads or learned new routes, and I was more tentative than I had been in the city. But the guide dog had always symbolized the final defeat, the end of hope, irreversible darkness. Proving that acceptance is never a linear process, even for an "expert," I resisted as if fighting for my last breath.

"I'm getting around just fine with the cane," I protested. "I go to work every day, I find my way in the city and I come home. Everything is all right."

"No," Jean replied. "It isn't. It's just irresponsible."

"We'll work it out," I insisted. "There's no need for such a radical step as long as I have some vision."

"But you don't, Luke. You really don't."

Walking home after the first snowstorm in December, I could neither tap nor sweep the cane from side to side, and lost the path repeatedly. Once again unnerved by not being able to find my way, and now numb with cold, I finally became more amenable to the idea of a dog. Jean had already done some research and learned that the Guide Dog Foundation, one of the best schools of its kind, was located in Smithtown, only ten miles away. I had spent over twenty years doing everything I could to postpone this day, but now it seemed that the sands had run out and I no longer had any choice but to submit, to relinquish any lingering pretense that I still had some "operative" vision. With Jean looking on, I drew a deep breath and agreed to make the call.

Twelve

WE SET OUT FOR SMITHTOWN IN EARLY JANUARY. A POWER-ful blizzard buffeted the car, sending swirls of snow across the road in what Jean described as a scene straight out of *Dr. Zhivago*. Excited by the storm as much as the prospect of getting a new dog, the boys laughed and whooped in mock terror whenever we swerved or skidded. By the time we arrived, the snow was already a foot deep, and they'd had a great adventure. But listening to the tires spin as my family drove away, I worried that they might not make it back.

Because it would be my home for the next four weeks, a staff member gave me a tour of the dormitory as soon as I got settled. "You won't be needing that," she said, taking my cane. "You need to learn to get around without it." Later, inching my way down the hall like a trepidant crab, I began to memorize the building, paying close attention to the location of different objects, smells, and how sound changed with any alteration to its environment. Within a few days I had begun to trust these as reliable markers, guideposts in the dark.

Since the blizzard ultimately deposited more than two feet of snow, the first stages of training were conducted entirely indoors.

173

Along with seven others, I was instructed on how to hold and assemble a harness, when to administer the different levels of correction, the intricacies of giving commands to a guide dog, and the importance of praise after a job well done. How fast we walked, how strong we were, our voices, and even our temperaments were carefully observed, the final assessments in determining the dog best suited to us.

On the fourth day we were brought together to meet our guides. This was the big moment, the one we had anticipated with increasing excitement. One by one, we learned the name, sex, and age of our dogs. I was to be paired with "Thea," an eighteen-month-old black Labrador. As if to prolong the suspense, we were directed to wait in our rooms until the dogs were brought to us.

Ten minutes later I held my breath as canine nails approached the door. Barbara Kaiser, one of the trainers, handed me a leash and suggested that I spend a few quiet minutes with my new guide. Thea sat calmly, licking my hand while I stroked her head. As I murmured her name I wondered whether this would work, whether I would be safe, whether I could really trust this dog to do her job. I had arrived at the moment I most dreaded, but had already begun to form a bond with Thea, the beginnings of a partnership.

Before rejoining the others, I recalled another escapade with Scoter, the first black lab in my life. In the same year I crashed into the Amagansett post office, I somehow got out of an outdoor playpen and began walking down the road. Shedding my clothes as I went, I headed west toward New York with Scoter by my side. My parents were terrified when they discovered that I had absconded, not least because there was a small pond next to the house. I had gotten pretty far before a farmer found us standing on the shoulder, a naked toddler out for a stroll with his watchful dog.

Thea lunged at the kids as they ran toward me on visiting day. Still growling while I held her back, there was no mistaking her protective aggression. Two of the boys began to cry before Barbara stepped in and took her away. While I supported the decision to pull her from training, I secretly felt a little disloyal, as if I had broken our covenant. Years later I was relieved to hear that she had been successfully placed with a woman who didn't have children. Stewart, a yellow lab of about the same age, was quickly introduced as her replacement, and it wasn't long before I knew he was something special.

The training process varies according to the abilities of each student, but generally consists of working with the dog in progressively complex circumstances. The first routes were straight lines, walking down a main street or through a mall, always under the close watch of a trainer. The courses became more difficult as our skills improved, and mastering each new challenge increased everyone's confidence.

Before starting on a walk through the town of Huntington, which would test Stewart's ability to navigate crowded sidewalks and my own competence at crossing streets, I issued a series of commands and got us to the front door of where we had stopped for lunch. As instructed, I told Stewart to sit before saying, "Forward."

He didn't move, so I said "forward" again. He sat perfectly still, and I heard Barbara begin to giggle. Frustrated and embarrassed, I said "forward" one more time, and once more he didn't budge.

Now laughing outright, Barbara said, "It might help if you open the door."

Stewart cut through the crowd with ease, weaving in and out like a motorcycle in rush-hour traffic. Barbara quickly intervened when a passerby asked his name and reached down to pet him, explaining that he was a working dog and should not be distracted. Turning to me, she stressed that keeping him focused when in harness would always be the key to our success.

Because the students shared many of the same hopes and concerns, friendships were quickly established. Our ages ranged from eighteen to sixty-seven, and we hailed from widely diverse backgrounds, but the need for camaraderie and support erased most of our differences. While some of this almost instant intimacy was attributable to the stakes being so high, we were also keenly aware that, once training was over, we would be on our own. Unlike when I was in Smithers fourteen years earlier, the prospect of "reentry" was one which, for a time, I was happy to defer. We were fully protected in this insulated world, a sensation most of us hadn't experienced in quite a while.

In the final week we set out to do a night walk on a course called "the backwards P," its name derived from how it appears on a map. In addition to darkness, a challenge for those with low vision, the route was longer than most and made more difficult by residual snow and ice. We were to walk alone, with no trainers hovering nearby to make sure we were all right. Stewart and I had been working well together, adjusting to each other's movements and idiosyncrasies. He was intuitive and highly alert, and I was beginning to trust him implicitly.

The night was cold as we set out, the chill prompting Stewart to walk faster than usual. Having practiced this route during the day, I was relaxed and didn't attempt to slow him. Crossing several streets before turning off the main road, Stewart took me around mounds of ice and slowed at slippery patches. Soon we were walking as if there were no barriers, nothing to hinder us. I let out a whoop and began to sing. "Yes, Yes, Yes!" I shouted into the night, and a classmate a few blocks ahead echoed my delight. I hadn't moved like that in years, absolutely free and unconcerned. We walked at nearly a trot, and I sang and danced with my dog. Leaving the foundation a few days later, I felt like nothing could stop me.

The next morning I came to a four-way intersection, with two lanes going in all directions. Before crossing I stood at the curb, listening to the traffic cycle. When the cars behind me began to move, I murmured, "Forward." Stewart stepped into the street, and we reached the far side without incident, exactly as it was meant to be done. Boarding the train, we arrived at work and reversed course at the end of the day. Within a few weeks Stewart had memorized my regular routes—home to work, home to the library, home to the store—and I felt no anxiety as we set out. I trusted him to do his job and, if I did mine, I knew I would always be safe.

Returning home on March 13, 1996, I stood up when the train cleared the sharp curve just outside the Northport Station. Stewart rose as soon as I moved, at once awake and eager, and we were at the door when it opened. The night was cold, with no wind. A brief thaw had cleared the sidewalks of ice, and the mounds of plowed snow which had blocked our straight passage down Larkfield Road had finally melted. Rush-hour traffic was jammed up on our left, and for a few minutes we outpaced the cars.

We turned on to Fifth Avenue just before seven, and I began to count off the five blocks to our house. Someone had a fire going, the wood smell instantly evocative of comfort and security. We were two blocks from home when tires screeched a short distance ahead. Before the car came to a stop I heard a mild thud, as if something small, insubstantial, had been hit. "Poor dog," I thought.

As we drew nearer I made out muted shouts, muffled cries for help. The sounds became more distinct as I crossed on to our block, alarmed voices and a car idling. Curious, I turned into our driveway and nearly collided with Jean.

"Something's happened," she said as she passed. "I think Christopher's been hit by a car. Call 911!" She ran into the street.

I found the house and went inside. Andy and Joe, then six, met me at the door. "What's going on, Dad?" they asked. "What happened?"

"I don't know, kids. I don't know, but I need to make a call." Andy ran into the kitchen and returned with the phone. My hands were shaking so badly that it took several tries to dial the three digits. "Hello," I said. "There's been an accident. My son has been hit by a car. No, I don't know the extent of the injuries. No. Listen, I'm blind. I don't know. I just got home. Please come quickly. Yes. My address is . . ."

"Dad, what's going on? Is Chris all right?" they asked again, and both began to cry.

"I don't know, guys, but I'm sure he'll be okay. The ambulance is on its way, and I'm sure he'll be fine."

They were crying uncontrollably now, and we huddled by the front door. Still in harness, Stewart circled nearby. I was anxious to get to Christopher, but how could I leave these two terrified boys by themselves? Finally concluding that I had no choice, I said, "Please listen. I know this is very scary, but I promise you everything will be all right. I need you to stay inside with the dogs while I go out to join Mom and find out what's going on. I'll send someone over, and I'll be back very soon."

"I want to go with you, Dad," Andy said. "I don't want to be alone."

"Me, too," Joe said. "I'm scared."

"I know, I know, but it would be best if you stayed here. I'll only be a couple of minutes. Promise me you'll wait until I come back."

They finally agreed, and I hugged them both. Heading toward the street I heard people yelling and an approaching siren. A radio crackled, confirmation that at least one police car was already on the scene. Jean came to me, grabbed my coat and said, "Oh, Luke. He's been hit, and he's not moving." Although she spoke softly, almost in a whisper, her voice sounded like a stifled scream. "Did you call 911?"

"Yes. Where is he? Why don't I hear him?"

"He's across the street," she replied. "By the tree. I don't think he's conscious."

We began to walk toward the opposite curb. People were standing on the sidewalk, and two men squatted in front of us. They spoke quietly to one another, or maybe to Christopher, but I couldn't hear what they were saying. Jean and I stood petrified, baffled, and paralyzed, holding on to each other. We didn't speak, uncertain and helpless. That I couldn't see my child nearly crushed me.

"Excuse me, sir, are you the father?" someone asked

"Yes," I replied. "How is my son? Are you a police officer?"

"Yes, sir. We're doing all we can for him."

"Why isn't the ambulance here yet? I called an ambulance. Please, you've got to help him."

As we stood in the dark another police car arrived, but still no ambulance. Christopher hadn't moved or made a sound. The night grew colder as the minutes passed. I strained to hear an approaching siren, but only the shifting of feet, an occasional cough, unintelligible conversations on the police radios, and people whispering broke the quiet. Jean and I stood over him, silent, dazed, unsure of what to do.

"Come and speak to him," one of the men kneeling by Christopher said, a trace of incredulity in his voice. "Talk to him. Maybe that will help."

Until that moment I hadn't realized that neither of us had rushed to hold or comfort our son, and was both shocked and ashamed. As if waking from a stupor, we knelt by him, still too frightened to touch his body.

"Hold on, Critter," Jean said. "Hold on. We love you, and you're going to be all right."

"Hang in there, little man. We're going to get you some help, and everything will be fine," I said. Because I couldn't see him I felt almost disassociated, far away. Standing up, I shouted, "Where's the fucking ambulance? Why can't you get an ambulance here?"

"It's on its way, sir," one of the policemen replied. "It should be here momentarily."

The ambulance finally arrived, more than twenty minutes after I'd called, and the technicians readied Christopher for transport.

Recalling that Andy and Joe were still in the house, Jean asked a neighbor to stay with them until we returned. I longed to comfort them, but we were ushered into a police car and followed the ambulance to Huntington Hospital.

When we sat alone in the waiting room, Jean said, "He wrote a letter asking the Cartoon Network to run his favorite show again. He wanted to mail it tonight, but I told him it could wait until morning, that it was dark and he wasn't old enough. I told him I didn't want him crossing the street, that he was too young. He said he was eight years old and needed to start doing things for himself. He promised to be careful. We argued about it but he insisted, and finally I let him go." She let out a gut-wrenching cry, and I turned to hold her.

"It's all right," I replied. "It's no one's fault. You did the right thing. He wanted to do it on his own, to grow up a little. You didn't do anything wrong."

A doctor approached. "Christopher is in very serious condition," she began. "He has suffered significant trauma, the full extent of which we don't really know yet. We're running some tests, but mainly trying to keep him stable. Our plan is to medivac him to Stony Brook hospital, since we just don't have the facilities to treat his injuries properly. I need to get back there now, but we'll keep you updated."

"Do you think he'll be all right?" Jean asked.

"As I said, he has suffered serious injury, but I believe there may be reason to hope. Stony Brook has an excellent trauma unit."

An hour passed, and Jean called our neighbor. She had taken Andy and Joe to her house, where they were sleeping. Doctors and nurses emerged periodically, giving us progressively vague and evasive news. Finally, around midnight, another doctor approached, and we stood up. "I'm sorry," she began. "We've done everything we could, but we just can't keep his pressure up. He can't be moved in this condition, and there's really nothing more we can do."

"Are you saying our son is going to die?" I asked.

"Yes, I'm afraid I am. We really did all we could," the doctor said, beginning to weep. "We all tried so hard."

"Of course you did," Jean said as the three of us held one another. "I'm sure you did."

I felt like I was floating in a madhouse, weightless and adrift, unable to right myself. The doctor's "yes" was like an explosion, its meaning too terrible to take in. Once again I couldn't speak, couldn't even cry, as if to give vent to emotion might break me forever.

"I'm sorry," the doctor continued, "but I need you to sign these forms allowing us to take him off life support. I'm so sorry."

"You're absolutely sure there's no hope for him, no chance for a life of any kind?" I asked.

"No," she replied. "I'm afraid not." Pausing, she added, "If you'll just sign these . . ."

Several people were weeping as we entered the examining room. I was surprised not to hear the sound of monitors, or machines of any kind. When Jean and I stood on either side of the bed, the staff left us alone. Bending over to kiss him, we said goodbye to our beautiful boy, holding his hands and stroking his hair.

After several minutes the doctor came in and stood behind us.

"Is he gone?" I asked.

"Yes," she replied.

"Goodbye, baby man," I whispered.

Footsteps approached as we gathered our things. "We'll take you home, Mr. and Mrs. Matthiessen," a voice said. It was one of the policemen who had brought us to the hospital hours earlier. Jean and I held hands in silence for most of the ride. The two policemen said nothing. There was nothing to say except what had already been said, and would be said hundreds of times again.

"I'm so sorry," they both muttered as we got out of the car. It was 1 a.m., and the temperature had dropped well below freezing. Although we spoke softly, our voices seemed to shatter the night.

Thanking them, I was deeply touched by their kindness, and that they had waited so long to take us home. The hospital staff had been especially caring, too, and suddenly this meant a great deal to me. I went upstairs to Christopher's room and stood in the doorway. Peering inside, the tears came at last, softly, almost as if I were afraid to wake him.

"Is Chris here?" Joe asked in the morning.

"Is he going to be in a wheelchair?" Andy asked.

The boys sat quietly while Jean and I explained that Christopher had died and wouldn't be coming home. They appeared not to comprehend the full extent of what was being said, as if the finality of death had no place in their lives. Like little Zen masters, they understood that Christopher had been with them, and now he was gone. They cried briefly at the news, but their thoughts soon snapped back to the present. I saw no sign of crippling psychological trauma, but by late adolescence Joe would be convinced he had accidentally hurt someone every time he drove, and Andy would be acutely attuned to any potential danger and overly protective of others.

We began to notify family and friends, starting with our parents. My father and Maria were away, so I left a message on the answering machine, hoping someone would pass it on. My mother arrived that afternoon, intuitively relieving Jean and me of the tasks we were already neglecting. Over the next few days her quiet steadiness and love held our lives together.

The phone rang constantly as word spread, and neighbors arrived to express their condolences. Some came with food, a few even putting money in our mailbox. Stationed in the living room, I alternated between answering the phone and the front door. We had little time to ourselves, but the relentless distractions weren't entirely unwelcome.

Jean astonished me by announcing that she wanted a wake, and we began to make the arrangements. Essentially agnostic, we were far less particular about the funeral. While we felt the need for a service of some kind, neither of us had any denominational preference or philosophical bent. Ultimately indifferent to doctrinal nuance, we were grateful when a friend said she would contact her Methodist pastor.

As I sat on the front step a man came up the walk and identified himself as a mechanic on his lunch break. He said he had read about the accident in the newspaper and was openly weeping.

"He was so beautiful," he said. "I have a son the same age. I can't imagine what you're going through. I'm so sorry." I thanked him, astounded by his selfless gift, and he went away without another word. Perhaps more than anyone else, that stranger personified the kindness we were shown.

"My arms are around you," Sidney Lumet said when he called, and I longed to run to his embrace. Larry wept in great bursts over the phone, repeating Christopher's name again and again.

Jean led me to the casket when we arrived for the wake. Straining to get a last glimpse of my son, I couldn't see anything in the dimly lighted room. Christopher's face was cold and oddly hard. Under the mortician's makeup his lips were curled slightly upward, as if in an incipient smile. Jean had asked that he be dressed in his regular clothes, and I made out a shirt and jeans. Scanning his body with my fingers, I drew a mental picture and filed the image in memory. Before returning to my seat I placed my lucky blue marble and his allowance, two dollars, in his pocket.

"I think we should go, folks," my father said as we readied for the funeral. Out of everything that was said that day, all the expressions of love and sadness, those are the only words I can still recall. Dozens of family and friends joined just as many neighbors and school teachers at the church. Joe LeSueur, who had been too upset to attend the wake, nearly staggered when he, my father, and Jean's two brothers carried out the tiny casket.

After the service it felt like the day had gotten away from us. The crowd was too large and reporters stood outside the entrance, confirming that saying farewell to our son had become a local media event. Jean and I even received a police escort to the grave site. Thankfully, only close family and friends accompanied us there.

We stood together as the final prayers were read, occasional gusts of wind chilling the sunny spring day. Jean collapsed after tossing a rose on the coffin, her entire body dissolving in sobs. "I'd never seen grief like that," Jonathan would say years later. "It was absolutely pure."

Several days after the funeral, the police informed us that we could retrieve what they had taken from the scene of the accident. While Andy and Joe played upstairs, Jean and I examined the contents of a large paper bag. I ran my hand over Christopher's boots and winter jacket, his glasses, the letter he had intended to mail, and the flashlight Jean had insisted he take with him. The jacket and letter were badly torn, the glasses frame bent and the lenses cracked. I taped the envelope as best I could and set out, glad to get some air and a few minutes to myself. Sensing my distress, Stewart was all but incapable of walking the two blocks to the mailbox.

As we struggled to find a way forward, I began to look for a sign that Christopher was somehow all right. Two mourning doves broke the quiet while I sat on the deck one warm afternoon, and I was convinced they had answered my call. A few days later, lying on his bed, I was hoping for similar reassurance when our cat, Blue, came in through the window. Still almost feral after being rescued from our back yard in Brooklyn, she had been affectionate only toward Christopher and hadn't been seen since his death. Jumping on to the bed, she curled up in the crook of my arm and began to purr. I chose not to dismiss this as coincidence.

Jean and I did everything we could to maintain a regular home life for our children, including celebrating their seventh birthday less than two weeks after the accident. Above all, we sought to reassure them that they were just as important as their brother and that their lives would go on, at least outwardly, as before. Jean sometimes set a place for Christopher at the dinner table, but usually took it away before the meal was served. We enrolled Andy and Joe in a bereavement group, but after three sessions they lost interest and we decided not to push it. They were much more excited about starting Little League, something I had foisted on an unenthusiastic Christopher.

One night in late April, after we put the boys to bed, Jean said she needed to speak with me. Only a few passing cars broke the silence as we sat together in the living room. Fumbling for a cigarette, she said she had debated whether to tell me about two remarks Christopher had made shortly before the accident, finally deciding that I had a right to know. She paused to inhale, then continued in quiet, staccato bursts.

Looking out the kitchen window in late February, Christopher had said, "I think I can see spirits in the sky. Sometimes I think I can see them in the clouds." Complimenting him on the beauty of this association, she hadn't given it another thought. A few days later he asked whether he might try a real coconut. When she brought one home he said, "Thank you, Mommy. I'm glad I had some coconut before I died."

My emotions raced from horror to grief, fear to guilt, separately and all together. It felt like a powerful hand had gripped my throat. And for a moment I couldn't speak. Neither of us had the courage to broach the terrible question. At last I assured her that his words had been arbitrary, unrelated, linked to his death only by coincidence, but they have haunted me ever since.

* * *

Sara Carey had done well in Minnesota. After her treatment, she settled in Minneapolis and found a job working as an aide on the psychiatric ward of a local hospital. She enjoyed her work and received high praise from both patients and staff, but had now been away for two years and wanted to come home. When she offered to stay with us, to help out in whatever way she could, we readied Christopher's room for her. She was marvelously funny and playful, the kids adored her, and she and Jean became close friends. Having her there was a blessing, a much needed counter-point to the prevailing sorrow.

Although they received a great deal of love and support from family, school, and friends, Jean and I never stopped worrying about Andy and Joe. How badly had they been scarred, were there problems we were overlooking, were we doing everything we could for them? They were forming some of their earliest memories, and we feared these would inevitably be laced with the indelible scent of funereal flowers, confusion, and inexplicable loss. I could recall only the good times when I was their age, and hoped that the gift of repression would do the same for them.

My mother-in-law purchased a small headstone, which was placed on Christopher's grave several weeks after the funeral. In addition to his name and dates, Jean had "Little Big Man" inscribed as his epitaph. I trained Stewart to find the stone and walked to the graveyard every weekend, stopping first to buy a single white rose. I always asked his forgiveness for ever having been harsh or insensitive, unaware or indifferent, finally thanking him for all he had taught me about love in our brief time together.

A few months after the accident Andy presented me with Christopher's toy cheetah. It had been his favorite animal, and I brought it to the grave to stand guard. When I returned, the boys asked, "Is he bones yet?"

Thirteen

S HORTLY AFTER RETURNING TO WORK, I LEARNED THAT THE
Bulova School was scheduled to close. Having befriended several social workers from a mental health clinic around the corner,
fellow commuters on the Long Island Railroad, I asked the director
if she would take me on. Talking it over on the eastbound train, I
agreed to a substantial pay cut in order to work as a therapist again.
It seemed a small price to pay for restoring a sense of dignity and
purpose.

"There's something you should know about me right off the
bat," Estelle said at the opening of our first session. She sat across
from my desk in a wheelchair, a hard edge in her voice.

"Go ahead," I said.

"I'm a stone-cold dyke."

In her mid-sixties, Estelle was dying of a degenerative neu-
rological condition. She had survived years of severe abuse as a
child, coping as best she could with alcohol, violence, and always
maintaining a hair-trigger toughness. Once assured that I wasn't
about to reject her, she began the slow process of coming to terms
with her life as a first step in preparing for death. Our weekly sessions began and ended with Estelle directing me down the hall as I

187

pushed her chair, Stewart attempting to guide us both. When she was too ill to come to the clinic I went to her home, where her partner welcomed me with a lovely lunch. Afterward I strained to write my notes using a black felt pen under a halogen lamp. No one mentioned it at the time, but I later learned that my charts were completely illegible.

"How fortunate that you have each other to help you through this," Jean and I often heard, but that was far from the truth. We had different needs and expectations after the accident, and were progressively frustrated by each other's inability or unwillingness to meet them. Once the initial wave of grief had passed, we began to withdraw from one another. Fragile and depressed, Jean kept largely to herself and the kids, and I did much the same. Rather than bringing us closer, Christopher's death intensified many of our old problems and ultimately widened the rift between us. I would later learn that 90 percent of marriages don't survive the loss of a child, and this came as no surprise.

By the end of the year, lonely and desperate for affection, I was drawn to Marcia, another therapist at the clinic. Her office was across from mine, and I gradually fell in love with the gentleness of her laugh and the warmth she showed her clients. Soon we were spending our lunch hours together, taking walks around the neighborhood, and getting to know one another more intimately. We began an affair, and I latched on to her love like a rescued castaway. Since she was also in a marriage which had lost its luster, we readily gave each other what we had long wanted for ourselves.

Marcia separated from her husband and rented a studio on the Upper East Side, where we rendezvoused twice a week. For a few hours we shut out our other lives and commitments, and in the morning walked separately from the subway to the clinic. In spite of our efforts to be discreet, I don't believe we were fooling anyone.

The first lover I had never seen, I imagined Marcia's looks from touch. Like an anthropologist reconstructing a face from a single shard of bone, I drew an image with my fingertips. She was never put off or disappointed by my blindness, never demeaned or resented me for it. I didn't feel particularly good about deceiving my family, but the empty and dispiriting alternative seemed far worse.

"I feel bad for her," my mother said after meeting Marcia. Both had wanted to accompany me to the hospital when I needed a hernia repair, and they had a chance to talk.

"Why is that?" I asked.

"Because she can't win," she replied.

Toward the end of 1997, Marcia informed me that the director's position at the addiction clinic in Brooklyn was vacant, but I was reluctant to apply. Since I was blind and had no management experience with the agency, I didn't see how I could possibly be a viable candidate. "You can do anything you want," Marcia said. Her repeated encouragement finally persuaded me to throw my hat in the ring, and she wasn't at all surprised when I got the job.

One of my Woodside clients, a Mexican psychic named Marina, presented me with an amethyst rock before I left. "It is for vision," she said, thanking me for my help in getting to some insights which had lessened her depression. The rock weighs about two pounds and is crowned with pieces of purple stone. I could make out its color under a bright light for a year or so, but now I just hold it from time to time, running my fingers over its jagged surface.

I managed the addiction clinic for the next seven years. The program treated some of the city's neediest men and women with medical, housing, and legal problems in addition to addictive and psychiatric disorders. As complex as the challenges often were, I flourished in my new job. It combined almost everything I believed would add meaning to my work—providing services to the marginalized, giving back to others in recovery, developing a highly effective program, and training newcomers to the field.

Known as "Mister Luke" to the clients, I did everything I could to help them feel important and valued. Whenever someone turned their life around, restoring a sense of self-respect and the potential for joy, I always felt we had achieved the highest fulfillment imaginable.

While many of those successes have now faded from memory, I will never forget Tanya, an HIV-positive prostitute who had come to the clinic after years of chronic addiction to crack. In and out of jail, she was homeless and had lost her kids to the child welfare system. By the time she completed treatment she had gotten a job, an apartment, and custody of her two sons. When I asked her to speak at the annual graduation ceremony, she accepted at once. "Of course, Mr. Luke," she replied. "Whatever I can do. Maybe my story will help someone else see that anything is possible."

* * *

The air conditioner muffled much of the hot July noise from Flatbush Avenue—buses, police cruisers, shouts, and boom boxes cranked up to window-rattling levels—but a passing fire engine made it difficult to hear my sister when she called. As its klaxon faded in the west, Sara Carey explained that our mother had suffered a brain aneurysm and was being transferred to Stony Brook hospital.

By the time we arrived she appeared to be doing well, stabilized and out of pain. They were draining her skull of excess fluid in an effort to reduce the pressure on her brain, the liquid dripping like a leaky faucet into a glass bottle by her bed. Her wits were as sharp as ever, and her doctor, whom she'd already dismissed as a "prig," told us that she had an even chance of recovering if she didn't have another rupture.

"Is my living will on my chart?" she asked. "I don't want these bastards doing whatever they want with me." Sara Carey assured her that it was prominently displayed. I called my uncle Archie, with whom she had always been close, summarizing what had happened and stressing that the pressure remained a serious concern.

My mother didn't appear to be overly anxious about her situation. That she didn't wish to live as an invalid or be in any way dependent on others was no secret, and I don't believe the specter of death in her seventieth year really frightened her. She was especially glad to see Archie and her sister Sarita when they came, their reunion calling to mind the third photograph she kept on her desk. In a small oval frame, the yellowed print showed her at age seven standing next to Archie, then five, who is clad in what looks like a dress.

Before the doctors could decide whether the potential benefit of surgery outweighed the risk, a second hemorrhage, larger than the first, nearly killed her. The doctors confirmed that she had suffered irreversible brain damage, and couldn't rule out another rupture. She was barely able to speak as I stood next to her, in the only space free of machines and tubes. Kissing her forehead, I began to reconcile myself to her dying.

Although our relationship had been complicated, we had never doubted each other's love. I would miss her warmth and humor, her energy and spirit, and the feeling of being home whenever we were together. Sitting on the deck later that night, I longed to fall asleep in the clubhouse with all three of my children, fish with Jackie, and have one last drink with my mother. Finally exhausted, I listened briefly to the darkness, crickets and a dog barking, a distant train whistle, and went to bed.

We arrived the next morning to find that the doctors had placed her on a ventilator, exactly as she had feared. As difficult as it was, Sara Carey, Archie, Sarita, and I quickly decided that her wishes should be honored and asked that it be removed. The staff complied without much resistance, possibly because Archie identified himself as an attorney. Each of us spent a few minutes alone with her, and we began to wait for the end. It came in the night, after everyone had gone. I chose not to "see" her body the next day, preferring instead to hold on to what Dick Seaver would later refer to as her "incredible vibrancy."

Mike returned from Italy and got drunk at the post-funeral gathering. "There's no one here I want to fuck," he said, scanning the crowd at the Benson Gallery in Bridgehampton.

"No one here wants to fuck you, either, Mike," I replied, and he howled with laughter.

The Bay Street Theater held a memorial at the end of the summer. Several friends and colleagues spoke, and two actors staged a scene from her play *Freddy*. Because I usually saw my Sagaponack siblings only on Thanksgiving or Christmas Eve, and never on my mother's turf, I was touched when Rue arrived. When a man approached with his wife and introduced himself as my old friend Steven, I was just as surprised and equally moved. We hadn't seen each other for more than two decades and discovered that we were both in recovery, I for sixteen years and he for six. Before parting, we pledged to stay in touch, but in spite of our drug-free connection—or maybe because of it—we drifted apart once again.

My mother's assessment of Marcia's dilemma had been prophetic. After two years she asked for more of a commitment, but I responded with a series of specious excuses as to why it wouldn't work. The truth was that I wasn't ready to leave my children, no matter how empty my relationship with Jean, not so soon after Christopher's death. In the end I left a good woman, extraordinarily loving and generous, and my guilt was only slightly assuaged when I learned that she had found someone else.

In the late fall Archie came with his son, Rick, to spread my mother's ashes. We chose her favorite spot on Louse Point in Springs, and took turns donning Rick's waders before tossing handfuls of ash and bone into Accabonack Creek. The day was sunny but cold, with almost no wind. We stood together on the shore when the plastic bag was empty, and Archie described a long line of ash riding the tide out to Gardiner's Bay.

Frank O'Hara's sister, Maureen, called several weeks later. She had purchased four plots in Green River Cemetery when Frank died, and offered the one next to his for my mother. I explained that there was nothing left to inter, but we agreed that she would have liked to be with him in whatever way she could. Her stone reads: "Patsy Southgate 1928–1998," but she had achieved Frank's "Grace to be born and live as variously as possible" as much as anyone, and it was fitting that they were together again.

For the next three years, our lives largely conformed to the schedules of suburban routine. I commuted to the city, the kids went to school, and Jean worked at *Newsweek* on Fridays, spending the night at a hotel after the layout was finished in the wee hours of Saturday morning. On weekends I walked to the grave, and we all went to Little League or school basketball games. Jean and I even attended a few PTA meetings, and I combined a speaking commitment at the 1998 RP Foundation conference with a trip to Disney World for the boys. While Andy and Joe were cementing the critical friendships of grammar school, Jean and I continued to grow apart, our grief and alienation superficially dulled by the daily rocking of the train and the narcotic effects of suburban living.

In early September 2001, about a week before the attacks on the World Trade Center, I went out to call Stewart in for the night. Darkness had brought little relief from the day's humidity, and mosquitoes buzzed around my ears as I waited for him. With no breeze I could hear my neighbor's television almost as if I were in his living room, but no rustling leaves or thudding paws. Still calling, I finally heard three "thumps" as he slowly climbed the deck stairs, and Jean noticed that he was favoring his back left leg. Thinking it was just a sprain, we went to bed.

The next morning he still wasn't putting any weight on the leg and now wasn't eating, never a good sign in a Labrador. Because I had an important meeting that day I decided to use my cane to get to work, and Jean agreed to take him to the vet.

"He's in agony," the doctor said when he called. "Believe me, any other dog would have tried to bite when I took the X-ray. He has a large tumor on that hip, and I'm afraid there's nothing we can do. We need to put him down, and the sooner, the better. I'm sorry, but there's no other choice."

"Please wait until I get there," I replied, unable to say anything more. We had gone on our long weekend walk only two days earlier, and Stewart had shown no sign of being in pain. Overcome by this display of stoic loyalty, I was devastated at the thought of losing him.

He was sitting on the examining table when I arrived, and I held him while the vet prepared the injection. He went limp within seconds. I eased him down as I burrowed my face in his neck, his warm dog smell briefly masking the room's antiseptic odor. Two weeks later the boys and I buried his ashes next to Christopher's headstone.

Suddenly without a guide, I had a renewed appreciation of the independence he'd made possible. Several schools said they would need six months to prepare a dog, but just as I was on the verge of panic the Guide Dog Foundation called back to offer a spot in the next class. Under Barbara's tutelage once again, I was paired with Mio, a bruiser of a black lab.

While it is always risky to assess the workings of one's own mind, I think it safe to say that in my earliest years I simply repressed painful events from conscious memory. By adolescence I had erected a kind of psychic wall, reinforced for more than a decade with plenty of alcohol. After getting sober, I could no longer banish unwanted thoughts to the realm of oblivion, but often remained disconnected from the feelings associated with them. Combat veterans sometimes describe this phenomenon as a kind of emotional shutdown, a disassociation which allowed them to go on.

Always present for my children and the clients at the clinic, I remained fundamentally apart from everyone else. It was as if I had formed an invisible shield, one which kept me at a "safe" distance, but also alone. When not with my kids or at work I was content only when reading or taking solitary walks, and found it difficult to relax in social situations. In spite of my training and experience, I hadn't detected the gradual onset of depression.

Andy approached as I sat on the sofa early in 2002 and put a hand on my shoulder. "Why are you so sad all the time, Dad?" he asked. His question jarred me. I had no idea I was so blue, far less that it might be obvious to everyone else. Assuring him that I was all right, I began to wonder whether the pervasive gloom was really the healthiest climate for the children.

In our separate ways, Jean and I did all we could for the boys, but I suspect that most of their happiness came from regular access to friends. I was terribly conscious of not being able to play catch, drive to the beach, or kick a ball around, and my attempts to compensate—walks, reading, raking leaves, or helping with their homework—didn't generate too much enthusiasm.

By now it was clear that my marriage was in serious trouble. Jean and I no longer pretended to be comforts to one another, and generally maintained a cordial but lifeless neutrality. Neither of us saw any hope of resurrecting what we'd once had, and even a revival of close friendship seemed unlikely. When I at last raised the possibility of divorce, five years after Christopher's death, she agreed that it was probably for the best.

"So, Lucas, you want out?" the mediator asked as soon as we sat down. The Grateful Dead played at high volume in the background.

Taken aback, I replied, "Yes, I think so."

Turning to her, he asked, "So, Jean, you want out too?"

"Yes," she said, her muted reply reflecting similar embarrassment.

"All right, then," he said, "let's get to it."

"Before we get started," I interjected, "would you mind turning the music down?"

"Oh, yeah, sure," he replied, nonplussed. "You don't like the Dead? I've got a lot of bluegrass. You like bluegrass? I love it." Pausing, he added, "Wait right here. I need to go take a shit. I'll be right back."

We had a good chuckle when he left the room. Remembering how often we had once laughed, I felt closer to her in that moment than I had in years. Until he returned and we began to "get to it," we exchanged a nostalgic fondness which briefly mitigated all animosity and bitterness. That night, after we had gone to our separate rooms, I recalled how, early in our relationship, I had taken her dog, Rufus, to be put down. In every way on her last legs, Rufus perked up upon entering the ASPCA, wagging her tail and bouncing down the hall, and I was repeatedly questioned as to why I had brought such a manifestly energetic and happy creature to be euthanized.

I wanted to be near my children but couldn't possibly stay on Long Island. With almost no public transportation, I would need to rely on Jean to drive me from place to place, and that just wasn't feasible. Since I worked in Brooklyn, I decided to begin my search in the downtown area, close to the main office and nearly all subway lines.

Before long I was shown a studio on Amity Street, an address I couldn't pass up. In the rear of the building, the apartment was quiet and small enough for a blind man to manage, and I agreed to take it. Because space was so limited, Joe suggested placing my tiny television in the fireplace. I was especially concerned with how the art was arranged. Since I could still visualize every piece, I wanted it to look just right. The Rivers lithograph would fit best above the mantel, Mike's seascape on the opposite wall, the Paul Davis nude above the bed, the O'Hara/Rivers collaboration in the kitchen, the Jack Youngerman *Paris Review* poster near the door, and the smaller pieces in the corners and bathroom.

196

The silence closed in after my family departed. I hadn't lived alone for almost twenty years, and never as a blind man. Nearly fifty, I didn't yet comprehend the full extent of how my life had changed, but recognized the first twinges of loneliness as I listened to unknown neighbors go up and down the stairs.

Amity Street was an ideal location in many ways. Not just close to work and travel, a supermarket, laundry, dry cleaner, fruit stand, veterinarian, and bank were all within a few blocks. I trained Mio to find each entrance by repetition and praise, simultaneously enhancing my own "mapping" of the area. Mio in harness was a canine magnet, and it wasn't long before I became something of a fixture in Cobble Hill, my new neighborhood. I hadn't experienced such a sense of community since my childhood on 11th Street, and having those connections, knowing those people were there, greatly eased my transition.

"You're so brave," I heard from some of my neighbors. I'd been told this before, but never so frequently.

"Thank you," I replied, "but I really don't think so. After all, what's the alternative?"

"Maybe so, but plenty of people don't get along as well as you do."

Despite the outward confidence with which I managed my daily life, my self-assurance was easily shaken in the first few months of independence. If I broke a glass I obsessed over picking it up, sweeping the floor again and again, worried that Mio might get a fragment lodged in his paw. If I didn't remember where I'd put my keys, it might be quite a while before I located them, groping with both hands over every flat surface. And if anyone moved something without telling me, it might be hours or even days before I found it.

It was never the larger challenges which forced me to seek the assistance of others. I could run my clinic, write reports, and travel to new places well enough; it was the little things—getting the television to work, finding someone on the street to read an address—which, unless quickly remedied, were most unsettling. Along with not being able to see the people I love most, this periodic helplessness has been the worst part of losing my vision.

At times I couldn't shake a conviction that I had abandoned my children. Although Andy and Joe looked forward to riding the train, sleeping on a futon, and having weekend adventures in the city, they were devastated when I told them I was leaving. Had I put my needs ahead of theirs, rationalizing that my absence would be preferable to a toxic home? No matter how I danced around it, I wasn't giving them enough time and had left Jean to deal with the daily parenting of two teenage boys. We had a lot of fun when they visited—going to movies, the Museum of Natural History, Coney Island, the Central Park Zoo, and John's Pizzeria in the Village, where I had often gone as a boy. With no restrictions on our mobility, we traveled everywhere by bus and subway. Doing so many different things with them helped me feel more like a regular dad, but I didn't believe I was sufficiently in their lives as a father.

While I had sworn I would never repeat his mistakes, the parallels to my own father were now impossible to ignore. I had two failed marriages and had left my children. I had been unfaithful to both wives and tended to see my concerns as being more important than those of others. I devoted a great deal of time and energy to my work, and my clinic received the Award for Excellence from the New York City Department of Health in 2002, but had others paid a price? Additionally, I was often guilty of manipulating situations and people to suit my convenience, a trait of his which had always angered me. Given all that, was I really so different?

George Plimpton died suddenly in September 2003. His memorial was held at the Cathedral of St. John the Divine, just south of Columbia and one of the few places in New York large enough to seat his many friends. "It was either here or Shea Stadium,"

Jonathan said, only half joking. My father read a marvelous passage from *Shadow Box,* one which confirmed that George could draw from the same well as the more critically acclaimed literati who filled the pews. Afterward we boarded buses which took us to Elaine's, and everyone had a grand party in George's honor.

Now in recovery for twenty years, I never felt like drinking but knew it probably wasn't wise to grapple with loneliness and a tendency toward depression on my own. As soon as I entered a meeting, the first I had attended in nearly a decade, I felt more centered and peaceful, less burdened. Welcomed and accepted at once, I quickly established important friendships. What resonated this time around were not the stories of drinking and getting sober, so important in my earliest days, but the insights about what got in the way of happiness and healthy relationships.

Uncharacteristically, I didn't rush into a romance as soon as my bachelorhood was official. Family legend had it that my grandfather couldn't be alone for more than ten minutes, and replacement wives had twice appeared with hardly a pause. My father, too, had always been partnered with someone, and never had to look too far to find a mate. Until now, my history had been much the same, with the result that I had twice entered into unions which, even before vows were exchanged, showed signs of fundamental incompatibility. Determined not to perpetuate that pattern, I made no commitments, worked hard, and spent as much time with my children as possible.

"We vacationed every summer in Noyac, near Sag Harbor. My father caught weak fish and kept them in a bucket until we went up to the cottage. I was little, five or seven, and used to name them. I felt so sad that they were going to die."

She had introduced herself to the group as "Claire" and usually sat in the row behind me. I'd had always thought hers to be a most beautiful name and began to pay special attention. Much as sighted people are initially attracted by appearances, I was taken with her voice. Soft and gentle, it promised both tenderness and passion. When she mentioned that she was a jazz musician, I was even more intrigued and eventually asked her out for coffee. Over large cappuccinos and a shared pastry, oblivious to everything around us, we began to reveal our histories with the excited anticipation of adolescents. Four years my junior, she was a classically trained bassoonist who had made the transition to jazz because she wanted to study improvisation.

"Hi Luke," she said when I ran into her a few days later.

"Oh, hey there," I replied, my thoughts suddenly racing. "What brings you to my neck of the woods?"

"Just picking up a few things at the store," she replied.

"Please, let me carry your bags. Really, I'd be happy to," I said, hoping this attempt at chivalry didn't sound too old-fashioned.

After several months, Claire confessed to having seen Mio and me walking down the street while looking out her window. Quickly slipping on shoes and a winter coat, she ran downstairs and followed. We were moving at our usual breakneck speed, so she had a hard time catching up. Finally intercepting us six blocks later, she pretended we had met by chance.

We fell in love and decided to live together. My studio was tight quarters for two people, a large dog, a cat, and a bassoon, but it felt like home to both of us. Regularly accompanying her to free jazz gigs, I learned to listen to music more acutely, to appreciate each instrument as an individual voice in a deeply personal conversation.

Claire suggested renting a tandem bike when we went out to Montauk that summer. She guided us all over town, calling back to tell me when to pedal or brake. And it wasn't long before we found a good working rhythm. By the end of the afternoon we'd had a thorough workout and much more fun than either of us had anticipated.

Anxious about swimming in anything but the calmest surf,

Claire began to trust that my ability to decipher the ocean's moods with my ears and legs would get her safely in and out. I held her hand as we stood in the shallows, timing the waves while determining the strength of both the undertow and any set running along the shore. Finally tightening my grip, I waited for the next wave to break as the last receded past our calves, and urged her to go. We ran together until, sensing the following wave beginning to crest, I let go and told her to dive, and we were safely beyond the breakers. She quickly learned how to catch a ride back to shore, but in rougher surf asked me to escort her in.

I hadn't seen Larry for more than a decade, but flew to Minnesota after learning that he had been diagnosed with hepatitis C. He moved as if weighted down, his voice slow and fatigued. Struggling to keep up a humorous front, his jokes couldn't mask his worsening condition. He returned to the Catholic fold when the end was in sight, not long after an unsuccessful liver transplant, and I flew back for his funeral. On the way home, I recalled him saying that he was perpetually anxious in New York and guilty in Minnesota, relaxed only at 35,000 feet, en route between the two. Intended to be funny, I had seen in his eyes that he meant it, and knew I would always miss him.

Larry had been the first to instruct me on program administration, and his lessons served me well. In 2006 I was promoted to "director of field operations," a lofty title which always puts me in mind of Field Marshal Montgomery but is far more modest in scope. In addition to the addiction treatment center, I was given oversight of a mental health clinic and several rehabilitation programs for the severely mentally ill. Told in no uncertain terms that I would need to master basic computer skills if I wanted the job, I went to Helen Keller Services for the Blind (formerly the dreaded Industrial Home for the Blind), where I learned to type and send emails. I had dodged technology for as long as possible, and wondered once again at the power of denial after seeing how a computer could expand my horizons.

Like my father, I was eager to show my children different parts of the world, and the added income allowed me to take them to Belize. Andy presented his elbow to guide me as soon as we met up, but Claire gently asserted her right to share in that responsibility. Even though she and the boys were no longer strangers, some familial adjustments were still in process.

Climbing the steps of a Mayan temple a few days later, I recalled the first time I had done it, when traveling with my mother and sister at age nine. After a short flight from Cozumel, two men in military fatigues met us at the end of a grass landing strip, both carrying rifles. Clambering into their open jeep, we drove down a dirt track toward Tulum, which was still being excavated. An iguana ran into the road and was immediately dispatched by the man in the passenger seat. Dinner, we guessed. Jungle still covered many of the buildings, but the skin of a large puma was stretched across one of the temple's steps. Reaching its summit, I was treated to a spectacular view of the Caribbean.

Traversing that same sea more than forty-five years later, we went to a small island for snorkeling and a beach picnic. I swam alongside Claire and shared in her snorkel-muffled excitement as she described a variety of tangs, angel and parrot fish, a moray eel peeking out from its hole, and a stingray fluttering across the bottom. After lunch, we were washing our hands in the sea when our guide began tossing chicken bones only inches away. As if on cue, a small lemon shark swam in to get them, snapping within easy reach of our feet. While obviously a practiced stunt for the tourists, its diminutive ferocity was as riveting as anything I'd seen in Australia.

While none of us lost any toes that day, Mike wouldn't be quite so lucky. He had miraculously made it into his eighties, but decades of too much drink, tobacco, and rich food had finally taken their toll. By 2007 he was diabetic, and his heart was failing fast. At the opening of his last one-man show he sat with a cane, never standing to greet his guests. He whispered that he was in a lot of pain, and it wasn't long before three toes were removed.

Claire and I went to Mount Sinai Hospital on Thanksgiving, joining his wife, Lynn Umlauf, and other friends for a makeshift dinner. We feasted together in I. M. Pei's atrium, sunlight warming the huge open space. Sitting in his wheelchair, Mike declared that it was the best Thanksgiving he'd ever had. He died of a heart attack in his studio on December 30th, not quite a week after his eighty-third birthday. "Goodbye, old paint," he had sung when I was a child, and I smiled at the recollection.

* * *

Mike had arrived in Springs with two beautiful roadsters, an iron green Bugatti and a royal blue Riley. Both had polished wooden dashboards with blue and yellow lights, and smelled deliciously of old leather and motor oil. The Bugatti was a large Italian sports car, and the Riley an elegant English sedan. Both had to be warmed up before driving, and the Bugatti made so much noise that the neighbors sometimes complained.

One morning, when we were four and three, Carey and I conceived a plot to send him away. Seeing that he had parked one of his cars directly below, we climbed out on to the roof, careful not to make any noise. We stood up slowly, holding onto each other, afraid but determined. At last we joined hands and, no longer able to repress small shrieks, jumped through the canvas roof of the Riley. Landing unharmed in the back seat, we were confident of success.

Several days later, after we were severely punished and the roof mended, he hadn't left and we knew our strategy had failed. The only choice left us was a direct attack. At dawn we ran into our mother's bedroom, jumped on top of him, and began pounding as hard as we could. He explained that our little knuckles hurt and

203

offered to buy us boxing gloves, and we agreed to put them on. For a few days we laced up before rushing in, but soon tired of it. He had won us over, and I'd had him for more than fifty years.

* * *

Remote and sullen after Mike's death, I sometimes snapped like the lemon shark. Claire tried to comfort me, but my unrelenting surliness wore her down, and she finally decided to leave. Desperate and alone on Amity Street once again, I feared I had driven her away for good.

After seven years, Mio was beginning to show signs of slowing down. Because guiding in an urban environment is more stressful, the working life of city dogs is generally shorter. I couldn't possibly fit another big lab in my tiny apartment, so my cousin Sally offered her Philadelphia home as his retirement paradise. With three other dogs and plenty of room to run around, he was sure to have a ball, as Mike might have said.

Arriving at the Guide Dog Foundation for the third time in March 2008, I was paired with Goose, a cross between a yellow lab and a golden retriever. In addition to his good looks, everyone reacted to his name, either praising its originality or condemning what they saw as its inappropriate silliness. He had been dubbed "Goose" by one of his "puppy raisers," Isabella Rossellini. Over his first year, she and Linda Larkin had taught him basic obedience while acclimating him to situations he would likely encounter when working—trains, buses, restaurants, offices, and the like. Ms. Rossellini has now raised more than ten dogs for the foundation, and was watching over a litter of nine pups when we met at her Long Island home. "Goose" was inspired by Gray Goose Vodka, that company having sponsored a film festival in which she was featured shortly before his birth. Being paired with a dog named for the substance which had nearly killed me, while certainly ironic, turned out not to be a bad omen.

Claire approached me in the subway after several months, her voice barely audible above the screeching wheels and deafening announcements. Before she boarded her train I asked her to reconsider, and she finally insisted on couples therapy as a prerequisite to reconciling. Stifling my resistance, I agreed, and we began the work which ultimately saved our relationship.

Aware that depression was fueling my irritability, I started to see another therapist once the couples work was over. After several weeks the theme of believing myself to be a fraud, so powerful in the final months of my drinking, rose to the surface once again. No matter how much the therapist challenged my thinking, I held on to the old conviction like a bulldog on the throat of its foe. At last he asked, "Whose voice is that?" While the obvious answer was probably a bit too obvious, and we both knew it, it was as if the spell had been broken. Just to know that I hadn't planted that seed was tremendously liberating, and we ended our work shortly thereafter.

Claire and I took Andy and Joe to Morocco after they graduated from high school, initially staying at a riad in Marrakesh owned by Maria's godson. It was a converted palace, and I especially enjoyed sitting on its roof as the Adhan, or call to prayer, rang out from four or five nearby mosques. The boys were thrilled to explore a foreign city on their own, just as I had done at their age, and Claire and I toured the nearly empty Jewish quarter and other ancient sites. The old city came to life as I listened to her verbal portraits and ran my fingers over carved stone.

Traveling through the High Atlas Mountains, we stopped to ride camels to the ruins of a hilltop Kasbah. When Claire's camel, Sha-la-la, got to his feet, thrusting her up and forward, she let out a whoop which must have been heard across the entire valley.

I proposed on a dark September 11th morning in 2009. Despite the solemn anniversary and rain clouds moving in from the west as we walked along a chilly beach at Montauk, I hoped the time was finally right and pretended to find an engagement ring in the sand. We arranged to be married the next summer on Amelia Island in Florida, not far from her father's Georgia home. A large sign was posted on the wall of the local marriage license office:

1. Are you over 15?
2. Are you related?
3. Have you been divorced within the last 30 days?

Along with my children and Claire's father and stepmother, the beachfront ceremony was attended by my father and Maria. My legs didn't shake this time, so my father remained comfortably seated while we read the following lines to each other:

Fragile ice whisperings
In clearest cold light
I come to you, and you to me
Grains of sand, gently
As soft as timeless
As the frozen reed, unseen
Silent and eternal
As inexorable as the intuited wind
On the day that has always been
–Luke

Seamless continuity
I have known you before
In other lands, other
Tide pools
Refracting sun rays
Bring forth the love

Found in a pomegranate seed
The dodos lumbered gracefully
Epochs ago
Beyond what was always known
–Claire

Our marriage hasn't been without its struggles, and occasionally the old demons reappear. But they are no longer welcome, and we quickly usher them away. While we can still squabble with the best of them, I usually catch myself before resorting to detachment, and she takes walks instead of threatening to leave.

Not too long before I stopped drinking, Joe LeSueur said to me, "Luke, what you need is a lesson in the three C's—charity, civility, and, most of all, compassion."

"Coming from you," I replied, "I must be in very bad shape indeed." I think I have made some progress in all three categories over the years, and don't believe for a second that Claire would've married me if I hadn't.

My blindness, while it is an essential part of our lives, as familiar as the touch of a hand or the morning's first kiss, remains a periodic catalyst for misunderstanding, defensiveness, and pain. When confronted with my inability to perform certain tasks I can still take out my frustrations on her. She misses the occasional acknowledgment of her beauty and the intimacy of eye contact, and it is only a growing appreciation of our shared dilemma which prevents us from hurting each other all over again.

More than anyone else, Claire has been responsible for quieting the voices of doubt and negation which can still whisper to me. Never resentful of my blindness, she has always challenged me with her generosity, patience, and understanding. Her gifts are many and, if I listen carefully, most can be heard when she improvises on the bassoon. Along with my children she has been the greatest blessing I have ever known.

My father was diagnosed with leukemia in late 2012. He had experienced extreme fatigue while in Mongolia, and the cancer was detected after his symptoms worsened. From the outset, barring a miraculous recovery, the prognosis wasn't good. While we held out hope that the chemo would work, it was also understood that, like any other drug, its efficacy would diminish over time. I hadn't confronted the possibility of his dying since nearly killing him fifty years earlier.

I was now sixty "years a' growing," and my father's illness brought my own mortality to the fore. I began to appreciate the importance of living each day as fully as possible, as something more than a vague abstraction. Closing in on senior citizenship, at one time an inconceivable milestone, I was delighted to reconnect with Jed Horne, with whom I'd largely lost touch after he'd moved to New Orleans in the 1980s to become the city editor of the *Times-Picayune*. In addition to countless newspaper and magazine articles, Jed had written two books and would be the first to suggest that I try my hand at a memoir. Jonathan came to Brooklyn and signed my copy of his book, *Studios by the Sea,* in recognition of our long-term friendship. I hadn't known until then that he had thanked me in the acknowledgments for introducing him forty years earlier to some of the artists profiled within. In light of my father's cancer and my children growing into manhood, renewing these old bonds was not just timely, but deeply gratifying.

Fourteen

"HE THINKS THIS WILL BE HIS LAST CHRISTMAS, MARIA whispered. My father had gone into his bedroom to rest, fatigued by the conversation and hoping to restore enough strength to see him through the evening's festivities. As I listened to my siblings and our children continuing to prepare for our 2013 Christmas and Hanukkah celebration, I was certain this would be the last time our whole patchwork family would gather for any sort of joyous occasion.

My father's voice had been strained, reedy, recalling Alex's aside at his eighty-sixth birthday party the previous spring: "He looks old, Luke, very old." Since I hadn't actually seen him for twenty years, this image was as difficult to imagine as the reality that he had shrunk significantly from his former six feet, two inches, or that he was unable to walk more than a few hundred yards without tiring, and not at all without the cane Claire and I had given him.

Although he had fainted several times as a result of dehydration or a low red cell count, a succession of transfusions had kept him strong enough to complete his last novel, *In Paradise*, while the chemo kept the cancer at bay. He had just informed us that the chemo had stopped working, and the cancer had returned. Now he faced the choice of trying an experimental drug or letting the disease run its course, which would likely result in death within two or three months. When I asked which way he might be leaning, he said he hadn't yet decided and shut down further discussion.

In the midst of the increasing clamor of gathering, preparation, and the younger children restlessly pacing near the tree, we stood silent, uncertain of what to do. I put my arm around Maria, but neither of us said a word. Claire attempted to buoy me with a half-hearted reminder that there was no way of predicting what might happen, but then fell silent.

Everyone was outfitted in their holiday finery. Eggnog was brought out, and the living room smelled of enticing kitchen aromas. I moved closer to the fire, as I always did in winter, glad for the warmth. Because Andy and Joe had been looking forward to seeing their relatives, I decided not to dampen their spirits with what I had just heard.

Maria suggested that Santa should make his appearance, surreptitiously placing a cowbell in my hand. I had amended the Christmas script for my Jewish nieces and nephew, and the sleigh bells and red barrel had long since disappeared. We decided to forgo the full upstairs routine, so I just stepped outside and gave it my all.

The frenzy of unwrapping was delayed until my father returned to "be in the bosom" of his family. This had become a favorite line in recent years, and we all laughed. The children opened their presents in a din of ripping paper and gleeful shouts, their parents admonishing them to place their gifts together with the accompanying cards so that appropriate "thank you" notes could be sent.

My father sat to one side of the fray, obviously drained, the noise and excessive materialism wearing on him. Perceiving that he might not have the energy to fulfill the role of host at dinner, I decided to give the welcoming toast. Speaking for everyone, I told my father that we loved and were with him. He had often expressed regret on this occasion about those who were not able to join us, and everyone understood that he was referring to my sister and Christopher. In more recent years he had not mentioned the missing, as time had dulled the pain of Christopher's loss, and it saddened him to reflect on my sister's unhappiness and his inability to change it. I saw no reason to resurrect their memories now.

Except for periodic phone conversations with Rue, Sara Carey was fully estranged from the family by the time we learned of the cancer's recurrence. She had declined dramatically since our mother's death, sealing herself off from even her oldest friends. I had coaxed her into joining Claire and me for Thanksgiving five years earlier, arranging to meet at a restaurant near her home. She was anxious and awkward, laughed inappropriately, and repeatedly referred to Claire as "Jean."

"How did you turn out so nice?" she asked toward the end of the meal. "You were such a shit when we were young." This escalated into a diatribe against my father, and I finally asked for the check.

When first informed of the cancer she expressed concern and love, but then sent a vitriolic letter blaming him for ruining her life. He was resigned to her absence, but still hoped to reconcile before it was too late.

"What's that old cliché?" he asked on one of our last walks, leaning heavily on his cane. "'You're only as happy as your unhappiest child?'"

But as the weeks went by and it became clear that death was imminent, she remained ensconced in her reclusive sanctuary. Not even Rue could prevail upon her to come when he entered Stony Brook Hospital for what everyone guessed would be the last time. I sat next to him while he slept, snippets of conversation filtering in from the hall while Alex and Maria whispered to one another in the slow quiet of waiting. Wondering whether I would ever see my sister again, I drifted back to an early morning long ago.

Under the slanted ceiling of our bedroom, the world outside

seemed suspended, inaudible, and shut away. The window was slightly open, a warm breeze just stirring the light curtains. We faced one another, a Noah's ark of stuffed animals on the bed between us. Endowing them with unique voices and personalities, we sent them on a series of animal adventures. My enormous lion and Carey's tiger counterpart held sway over our animal kingdom, and they always remained friends.

A doctor entered and declared that my father could be discharged. "We're taking you home, Dad," I said when he stirred.

"Indeedy," he replied. In his condition this response was almost heroic, but I didn't appreciate the irony of his last word to me until several days later.

An ambulance carried him back to Sagaponack, and I returned to the city. Alex called late that evening to say that his condition had taken a precipitous turn.

Approaching Bridgehampton the next morning, I remembered how one had to walk down four or five steps from the old trains to the platform. There were no ramps, handrails, or ticket machines. A lumberyard abutted the station on its eastern end, a sign painted on its side. The understated smells of railroad ties and creosote settled over the platform after the diesel fumes had dissipated, the quiet and dusty rural setting somehow suggestive of Faulkner's Mississippi.

Only a handful of people would have disembarked on April 5th. No taxis would have been waiting, and several minutes might have passed before a car drove by. He usually asked that I call from the pay phone when I arrived, in case the train was late. Waiting for him, I listened to the fading whistle and bird calls on the wind.

"Hello, hello," Rue said to Claire and me as we completed our winding descent of the ramp and parted from the Hamptons crowd.

"Hello Rudy," I said. "Is there any news?"

"It definitely looks like today," she replied. "He had a hard night, and Linda doesn't think it will be long now." Linda Coleman, a hospice nurse, was one of my father's Zen monks and had been attending him regularly.

I pictured the route as we drove toward the house, pinpointing our location by the car's movements and the heartbeat sound the tires always made on Ocean Road. When we turned on to Bridge Lane, I opened the window to let in the unseasonably warm air. The car descended the hill toward the creek where Sara Carey and I had gone crabbing as children, bumping on and off the small bridge as if nothing had changed over the past five decades, and we were in Sagaponack.

"Hello dears," Maria said. "I'm so glad to see you." Her speech was fatigued but strong, resigned, with only a trace of uncertainty and confusion in its cadence.

"How are you holding up?" I asked.

"It's been difficult," she admitted. "We didn't get much sleep and weren't sure he would last until morning, but I'm all right." If there had been a crack in her stoic demeanor, forged over the course of her British colonial upbringing, I hadn't seen it yet. My stepsister, Sarah Koenig, emerged from the kitchen, her embrace still as loving as that of the five-year-old who had first joined our family more than forty years earlier.

Alex was in the bedroom, speaking softly with Rue. Claire gave my hand a squeeze, and we went inside. "Hello, Luke, it's Michel." Michel Engu Dobbs was another of my father's monks and had recently been designated to succeed him as Roshi of the Ocean Zendo. He was a warm and kind man, and I was instantly soothed by his presence.

My father lay on the bed, his breathing slightly labored. He exhaled with a plaintive moan, as if distressed, a fading cry not unlike the last note of the mourning dove's call. Linda entered the room and declared that all was as it should be.

"Is he in pain?" Claire asked.

"No," Linda replied. "What you're hearing may be his way of comforting himself."

I sat on the bed and found his hand. "Hello, Dad," I whispered. "It's Luke. I'm so glad you're home. It's a beautiful, warm day. Spring is here, as I'm sure you can tell." His hand rested in mine, unresponsive, and there was no change in his breathing.

"You've had a wonderful life, Peter," Kurt Vonnegut had said at my father's reading from *Birds of Heaven* in 2002. Sitting with him on his last day, I hoped he appreciated not just that sentiment, but all he had achieved. Never one to rest on his laurels, he was always pondering what else he could do to keep the world's attention on the crimes we continued to perpetrate on the planet and each other.

For most of his adult life he had also been plagued by a conviction that he would never be recognized as a fiction writer on a par with his friends and peers, that he had been forever pigeonholed as a nature and travel writer, or that posterity would remember him only as the author of *The Snow Leopard*. Winning the National Book Award for *Shadow Country*, a reworking of the three Watson novels into one, not only helped to mitigate his fears regarding his legacy as a novelist, but also earned him the special distinction of being the first writer to have received the prize for both fiction and nonfiction. Only since the cancer's recurrence had he begun to reflect on his accomplishments with an occasional hint of pride. "Thirty-one books," he mused one afternoon. "That's pretty good."

Shortly after he began a trial of the experimental drug which quickly ended his life, I sat with my father while he reclined on his bed. As indistinct voices floated in from the living room, he revealed that, not long before his death in 2000, my grandfather had acknowledged him as a "great man." I had understood previously that he had said nothing more than "Good luck with your projects, Peter." While glad to hear that he had at last received the paternal sanction which had so long eluded him, my father's recounting of that moment seemed out of character. He was rarely one to boast, and I don't believe he would have repeated this were he not coming to terms with his life and forgiving those who had wronged him.

"To be recognized as a great man by him must have meant a lot," I said, but he didn't respond. I didn't ache for similar acknowledgment, since I had come a long way toward accepting myself for who I was, no more and no less. At my best I might be "a terrific guy doing great things," as he had said after visiting one of my clinics, and would be foolish indeed if that weren't good enough.

As his final morning passed into afternoon, everyone took turns sitting by the bedside. Claire and I went for a short walk in the sun, and I realized I would probably visit this house only once more. Without knowing what his wishes were, I assumed that a memorial of some kind would be held here in the next few weeks, but there would be no reason to return after that.

When his breathing slowed and he ceased to moan, Linda quietly announced that he would die soon. Claire put on a recording of Mozart wind concerti, the perfect accompaniment to the sounds of spring. "Tell him that it's all right to let go, that all is well and he can be at peace. He should know that he doesn't need to hold on for any reason," Linda said.

We began to speak softly to him, taking his hand or stroking his head, and Michel lit some incense. "It's all right, Dad," I said. "I love you. You can rest now, let go. I'm all right, we all are."

Linda suggested that someone get Maria. His breathing became more shallow and continued to slow. My siblings' voices grew louder, more urgent.

Unable to see my father's dying, I sat upright and listened. Murmured prayers, the movement of my family closer to him, love and fatigue in their words, the room filling with audible anticipation. With a crescendo like that of approaching geese, the tree outside his window came alive with song, dozens of birds calling as if in a single voice, a cacophony I probably would have missed had I not been paying attention.

The birds sang and Mozart played softly. Small gusts of wind came in through the window, promising a chilly night. "Goodbye, Dad," I whispered.

After nearly a minute Alex asked, "Is he gone?" The birds had flown away.

"Yes, he is," Linda replied.

Each of us stood alone for several seconds before we came together, weeping and embracing one another. Huddling over his body, the differences in our parentage, ages, and personalities, the unavoidable jealousies and resentments of children brought together from disparate homes, were momentarily put away. We loved each other without reservation in our grief, but such closeness wouldn't last.

Maria entered, and we moved aside to let her sit by him. The room was silent except for a blending of Mozart and birdsong on the wind. Taking a deep breath, she said, "A mighty oak has been felled," her words resonating in the ensuing quiet.

I stood on the opposite side of the bed, looking down at where I thought his head ought to be. Without being able to see him it was difficult to accept that he was no more. Larry Rivers had described Frank O'Hara's body in extraordinary detail, and now I understood why. I would have given almost anything to look at my father, to see his death, but touch and imagination would have to do.

"It is a Zen tradition to wash the body, so Linda will give each of you a damp cloth, and then we will chant the Heart Sutra in memory of Roshi Peter Muryo Matthiessen."

Since I was standing at the foot of the bed, I began to wipe his leg. Michel distributed the text of the Sutra, and everyone took turns between chanting and washing him. Claire stood on my left and bathed his upper torso. As my family chanted in 4/4 time, the room was suffused with the subtle aroma of Japanese incense.

First Light

KAN JI ZAI BO SA GYO- JIN HAN-NYA HA RA MI TA JI
SHO- KEN GO ON KAI KU- DO IS-SAI KU YAKU
SHA RI SHI SHIKI FU I KU- KU- FU I SHIKI

The ritual over, everyone but Michel left the room. Maria rejoined two friends who had waited outside. Andy and Joe arrived, upset over having been delayed in traffic, and went to say their final farewells.

While others began to notify family and friends, coordinating plans and schedules, I returned to the bedroom when certain of being alone. After sitting next to him for the last time, I held his hand and ran my fingers over his face. Imagining how he looked in the quiet aftermath, I was filled with gentle sadness. I felt the sorrow not of extinguished hope, but that of genuine loss.

Closing my eyes, I pictured the whale's great flukes as they swam toward the sky. His hair was gone, lost in the battle against cancer, but I wondered whether he looked more like a newborn than his bald father. Just as people had sometimes mistaken my voice for his when I answered the phone, others had begun to say that I now resembled him.

Mixed with the sorrow was a profound sense of relief, and even a tinge of joy. Not for the fact of his dying, but in knowing that his suffering had ended and I had finally exonerated him, as he had long since forgiven me. Before his death, I had found a way to love him for all he was, and wasn't, and he had done the same. I had let go of my lifelong demand that he be someone else, just as he had abandoned his narcissistic desire to cast me in his image many years earlier. He had been pleased when I predicted that *Shadow Country* would one day be recognized as a classic of American literature, perhaps sensing that I had at last made peace with the reality that his work always had to come first. In the end, neither of us had been castrated or killed, and letting him off the hook had freed me for good. He had done his best, and so had I. Like him,

217

I knew I had my shortcomings as both a son and father. But I was also certain that, again like him, I had never been feckless when it came to my children. Even so, I think he would have agreed that we all could have used a little more affection from our "ever lovin' Dad," as he had always signed his letters.

I opened my eyes and sensed that the day had dimmed. Sarah was exhorting everyone to join her on a walk to the beach while the undertaker came to collect his body. In the final minute of our time together the tears returned and I stroked his shoulder before closing my hand over his. I felt a release, a final easing of tension, and a solitary mourning dove called out from the west.

Almost twenty years earlier the image of my son before a fountain had appeared like a few unspoiled frames in an otherwise ruined movie reel. I glimpsed his profile in silhouette against the bright, cascading water for just an instant. His head slightly bowed, His forearms were raised as he shook them, his fingers spread wide. Barely audible beneath the tumult, I could just hear him, his little chirps of joy like music. Unaware of anything but his image encased in sound, I held him in my sight for a few seconds, forever, before he disappeared again into the darkness. "I did that as a little boy, too," my father said as he observed his grandson one afternoon. "Exactly that motion." Laughing, he added, "Maybe it runs in the family."

We walked to the beach at twilight, the temperature falling with the sun. Emmett, Rue's only child, threw rocks into the sea while the rest of us stood by like a flock of loosely congregated gulls. The shore he had come to for more than half a century seemed almost foreign, unfamiliar, as if not having him to point out different birds or a tern's nest had somehow altered the landscape. With night coming on, Claire and I linked arms with Maria and, in silence, turned toward home.

Like we had done after the Christmas Eve festivities, my family returned to Brooklyn. Heading west we said little, quieted by the headlights, the rhythm of the road, and the futility of attempting to articulate as yet unformed thought.

"Oh, my God," Claire said out of the silence. "Peter's obit is in the *Times*."

"That didn't take long," I replied, as dismayed as my father might have been to learn that his death was already a media "event," and that we weren't to be allowed even a few hours of private mourning. Pushing my bitterness aside, I told myself it probably couldn't be helped and, ultimately, didn't matter.

In the weeks following his death, Maria assumed the Herculean task of organizing, cataloguing, and cleaning out the contents of my father's office. Each child was then presented with a bag containing notes, drawings and other papers particular to them, collected by him in the bottoms of drawers and filing cabinets over the decades. A small tin containing his ashes was also packed into each.

Looking through its contents, Claire and I discovered a ceramic figure of a man in a boat. I had made it for him when seven or eight, and recalled every detail with my first touch. The man's black hair resembles a toupee, and he is dressed in blue. The boat is brown, and his arms are resting on the gunwales. His eyes and smiling mouth are indented into an almost perfectly round head. Like his shoes, these are painted black. We placed it on a shelf alongside the small tin.

Among the papers, Claire found the letter I had sent my father after returning from Africa. I listened carefully as she read, remembering the graceful leap of a Thompson's gazelle, the red robes of the Masai, and driving across a dusty Amboseli Plain. Looking up when she finished, Claire said I looked as if I had been dreaming. The letter ends: "I miss Africa more than I can say. Each day I miss it more. The whole time I felt like I was the first man to ever see it. I want to go back now, just us. That would be the ultimate appreciation of it. Thanks and I really wish I could see you. I really miss you, Dad."

Hearing these words more than forty-five years after they were written, I was struck by how I referred to myself as a "man" at the age of fifteen, and how much I yearned to have my father to myself. I can only speculate on what prompted this sentiment, but I believe Africa was the key. Watching in silent awe as thousands of wildebeest passed before us on their annual migration, or listening to the far-off cry of the hyena as we lay in the night stillness of our bungalow, we were somehow removed from the "real" world and the past associated with it. We were together in a way we had never been, and we never realized such unfettered intimacy again. I had him in Africa, and he had me, but the note hints at an understanding that we had come as close to the "ultimate appreciation" of each other as we ever would, and that this could only have happened in the short time we spent together in paradise.

Fifteen

A CAR PASSED, NO SOUND OF WET TIRES. I WASN'T AWARE OF truck noises or horns, not even in the fading preconscious memory of awakening. Although both windows were open, it was surprisingly quiet. The garbage trucks had taken the night off, and birds could be heard in the intervals between city sounds.

Climbing into full consciousness, I oriented myself to the day. The electronic rooster crow of my "talking" watch hadn't sounded, and I remembered that today was the Fourth of July. I turned toward the windows and scanned the blinds with ritualistic precision, hoping to glimpse any sign of light.

The almost indiscernible glimmer vanished as soon as I had seen it. Working backwards I again detected the dim flash, confirmation that the sun was up. Claire placed her hand on mine. "Hello, baby," she said, her voice soft with sleep.

We kissed and I got ready to fulfill the first of the day's duties. As always, Goose was poised by the side of the bed, panting in anticipation as he waited for me to stand, the signal that he would soon be fed. I rose and he charged ahead to the kitchen, slipping on the wood floor as he went. With one hand held in front I followed and found his bowl.

Five minutes later I returned with two cups of coffee, both elbows slightly outstretched, in case I veered into a wall.

"Happy Louie's birthday," Claire said as I handed over her cup. Although he was actually born on August 4th, Louis Armstrong always claimed to share the nation's birthday. WKCR, the radio station of my alma mater, honors Satchmo every year by playing his music all day on both dates. This is always a double treat for us, but especially for Claire, who loves Louie above everyone else. "Let's go see the fireworks tonight," she added.

The show was to take place over the Brooklyn Bridge, so the display from anywhere in our neighborhood was sure to be spectacular. In spite of my love for her and our many years together, a vestige of old anger briefly fought to rob this prospect of its pleasure, to ensure that she wouldn't see any more than I. "Of course, honey," I said. "It will be fun."

Sipping my coffee while Claire showered, I thought of how fortunate I had been to find her, and how much her love meant to me. Certain we were now partnered for life, we both knew our best years were yet to come. My kids were out on their own, discovering their separate joys and struggles, doing fine. Since I had also been given oversight of two more clinics and close to two thousand people now received services from programs under my supervision, I had realized a vocational fulfillment I'd never thought possible.

The subdued sounds of the city on holiday wafted up from the street as I looked toward my future. That I was still in good health at sixty-one was nothing short of miraculous, and I didn't much fear the coming infirmities and gradual declines of old age. I was content with my life, what I had finally made of it. Fully appreciative of how important mentors had been, it was especially rewarding to know that several others had now assigned that role to me.

I got up and turned on the radio, sure this would elicit a whoop of delight from the bathroom. Louie's voice filled the apartment, and I was instantly caught up in his exuberance. Singing along to

"I Get a Kick Out of You," I recalled Renee's warning about the insidious allure of alcohol and, almost simultaneously, an afternoon at Hazelden nearly thirty years earlier.

Jerry was my first client on the extended care unit. Tall and almost gaunt, he wore thick glasses and had lost most of his teeth. Originally from Louisiana, he had lived the life of a hobo for many years before coming to treatment. Jerry didn't remember much of his childhood, but I learned that he had been raised in a wealthy home and was eventually found by an estate attorney in a hobo village. Because he had suffered significant brain damage as a result of his alcoholism, he had been sent to Minnesota by his legal guardians.

Working with Jerry was fascinating. He loved to relate details of his life on the road, which included riding the rails and straining shoe polish through bread when he and his companions had nothing else to drink. He came alive when discussing his past, sometimes sounding almost wistful. One day I accompanied him on an outing to a local shopping mall. Before going inside we heard the whistle of a far-off freight train. Jerry turned toward the sound and halted, saying nothing. The tears came, and he paused for another moment before moving on.

"Let's make the bed," Claire said.

Looking up at the fireworks a few years earlier, I'd seen a flicker of green, bright and unmistakable, and my heart had soared. The luminescent emerald burst had remained in memory, a fleeting but powerful connection to what had been. Maybe tonight, with the shells going off practically over our heads, I might be treated to another reminder of color. But since it wouldn't be wise to get my hopes up, I told myself that it would be enough to share in Claire's delight.

I got ready to go out for bagels, and called Goose to the door. First attaching the leash, I put on the harness and noticed that it had gotten tighter. He was older now, close to retirement and prone to weight gain. "Find the elevator," I murmured and he did so without hesitation

"Excuse me," I said minutes later to footsteps passing by, "can you tell me if there's a trash can on this corner?"

"Yeah, right over there," a man replied.

Trying not to sound too exasperated, I said, "I'm sorry, but I'm blind and I don't know where you mean when you say 'over there.'" After working with guide dogs for eighteen years, I am only a little less surprised by the occasional thoughtlessness of others. While I've gotten better at not showing my frustration, I found myself thinking, *I'm standing here with a dog in harness, a bag of shit in my hand and I'm asking you to help me find a garbage can which probably isn't more than ten feet away. You don't know I'm blind, you idiot?*

"Oh, yeah," the man said. "It's about five feet forward and to your right."

"Thank you," I replied, reminding myself to be kind.

I guessed he was on his phone and oblivious to everything around him. When cell phones first came out and I heard people say, "Hello," as they approached, I usually responded with a cheery "hello" of my own. For a time I marveled at the sudden friendliness of New York passersby, and felt foolish indeed when I finally realized what was happening.

We crossed two more side streets before coming to a busier corner. "Left to the curb," I said, and Goose found the crosswalk at once. I wasn't sure whether this was attributable to his diligence, or simply the result of having traversed this route innumerable times. I praised him in any case, a little guilty about not having done the daily obedience training in over a week. Now on the Guide Dog Foundation's board of directors, I surely wasn't its best representative.

That night we went to the roof of a tall building not far from the Brooklyn Bridge, a home for seniors operated by the agency.

Entering the building with my third guide, I felt like an old-timer in my own right.

Claire and I joined about thirty seniors, some in wheelchairs or accompanied by aides, and soon found ourselves talking with the residents. How "pretty" Goose was dominated most exchanges, and I violated another cardinal rule of guide dog handling by allowing everyone to pet him. After a few minutes we all settled down, waiting for the show to start.

I stared straight ahead, at what I guessed was the southern tip of Manhattan. Horrified, Claire had watched the south tower come down from the Brooklyn Heights Promenade, almost directly below us. Like the footage of the planes crashing into the towers, or people jumping from them, images indelibly etched on the sighted American psyche, I wasn't sorry to have missed what she had seen. Closing my jacket against the chill, I recalled a special day with my son Joe.

The street throbbed with sound, car horns and piercing sirens, the roar of diesel engines, men yelling to one another, radios crackling in the hot September air. On September 16th, 2001, Joe and I emerged from the subway at Canal Street and stood before a line of police. Holding my cane in one hand and Joe's elbow in the other, I squinted against the glare which still pained my sightless eyes. I identified myself as a social worker and informed a policeman that we had come to help in whatever way we could. After a brief exchange he paused and asked us to wait while he consulted his commanding officer.

Despite repeated assurances over the previous four days that there were already more than enough volunteers on the scene, and hints that a blind man and a young boy might prove to be more of a hindrance than anything else, Joe, then twelve, remained convinced of where our duty lay. When on Sunday morning he again asked me to go, I couldn't deny his wish.

The police officer returned and suggested we go up to the Javits

Center on 34th Street, where the first responders were taken after their shifts.

In another minute we were introduced to a supervisor from the Department of Buildings, and Joe was thrilled to get a ride in an official car. We began by making "care" packages for the ironworkers and firemen, which included eye drops, moist wipes, throat lozenges, and granola bars. I alerted a doctor in charge that I would also be available to meet with anyone seeking counseling, and was told that buses from the site would be arriving in an hour.

We quickly developed our own assembly line technique as we sat in the sun. Although I barely moved, I was sweating profusely and soon felt the top of my head beginning to burn, confirmation that I was balding more than I cared to admit. Following Joe's example, I didn't complain.

A man approached and introduced himself as a police captain. "Was this your idea, son?" he asked. After Joe replied that it was, he added, "Well, you're the youngest volunteer I've seen, and I tip my cap to you."

"Dad, he actually took off his hat," Joe gushed after the captain had gone, a proud smile in his voice.

It wasn't long before several buses pulled up and heavy footsteps approached.

"May I help you?" I asked. "Please have a seat."

"Do you have an aspirin?" a man whispered, his voice shaking.

"Of course," I said, handing him a packet. "Are you all right? Would you like to talk?"

"I can't go back down there," the reply came at last, thick with exhaustion, quiet and vacant, undirected.

"Sir," I said, "please sit down. Let's talk. Maybe I can help."

"I need to go home," the man responded. "I can't go back down there."

I stood up and moved toward him, offering my hand. "I understand," I said. "Please sit with me for a minute."

He began to sob. Slowly walking away, he repeated, "I need to go home. I need to go home. I can't go back down there," and he was gone.

Staring blankly in his direction, I pictured a large, dust-covered man shuffling toward Penn Station. Had my blindness been a barrier? If I had been able to make eye contact, taken his arm, or even walked with him, could I have helped him to talk about it? In nearly thirty years of practice this was the only time I experienced my blindness as a possible handicap. Even though my more rational mind understood that he probably needed a lot more than I might have provided, sighted or not, just after returning from hell, I couldn't let go of a suspicion that it might have been different had I been able to see him.

After we had assembled innumerable kits and it was clear that no one else would be coming for counseling, Joe announced that he, too, wanted to go home. The heat had taken its toll, and I knew we had probably done all we could for one day. Praising him for his spirit and tenacity, I added that this was the best Sunday I'd ever had.

The show from the Jersey side started shortly after nine, distant but apparently impressive, and our collective excitement began to rise. An old man sitting next to Claire initiated a discourse on how pyrotechnic displays were orchestrated, and I remembered a year when George Plimpton began his annual show by shooting off one shell at a time, prefacing each launch with a brief explanation of what we were about to see—the particular characteristic of the firework, its construction, and its country of origin. I was fascinated and charmed, captivated by the intimate enthusiasm of his presentation and how it contrasted with the overkill of the larger displays, like the one we were about to experience. Thirty-five years later, I smiled at the recollection of George's boyish pride when Mayor Koch appointed him the Fireworks Commissioner of New York City.

The older people were increasingly animated, a testament to the power of pyrotechnics to excite and even transport, no matter our age or how many times we've seen them. Claire and I were grateful to have happened on such an extraordinary vantage point, and I was glad I hadn't cast a pall over her eager anticipation. Below us hundreds of thousands had gathered along the waterfronts of Brooklyn and Manhattan, many having secured their spots hours earlier. A muffled crescendo of horns and cheers rose up to the sky as everyone awaited the big event.

Suddenly there was the unmistakable "vhump, vhump, vhump" of many shells being launched from below, and the air was filled with sound. Shells were exploding overhead and all around us, set off from barges on the East River and the bridge itself. Claire stood up at once, but I remained seated and began my search for any semblance of color. In contrast to the din in the heavens, the old people made almost no sound, their presence felt only by stifled gasps or polite clapping.

The show roared on, the air choked with noise and the smell of gunpowder. I was certain I would see something, probably couldn't help it. Surely some anemic rod or cone cell would fire a signal to my waiting brain. But while others cheered and "Oohed," I could see nothing but undefined and fleeting evidence of the sky getting brighter. Nothing specific, and nothing in color.

"Can you see anything?" Claire asked.

I sat rigid, my eyes fixed on one spot, believing I had a better chance of seeing if I didn't move. Some sort of image had to emerge, even in my nonexistent field of vision. Debating whether to throw out a lie so as not to sadden her, I replied, "No, nothing yet. Am I looking in the right direction?"

She crouched behind me, clasped my head in both hands and slightly redirected its position. "There. That should do it," she said. "It's right in front of you."

I stared straight ahead, willing myself to see. Until then I hadn't

First Light

realized how much weight I had attached to this moment. Although I couldn't say it to Claire, could barely acknowledge it to myself, I knew that, if I couldn't see anything under these circumstances, I would never see again. An occasional source of light, perhaps, but that would be the extent of it. The night was cold for July, but I began to sweat.

The show lasted for almost half an hour and featured sound effects I had never heard, including long cracklings which were meant to complement the multicolored wave effects Claire described as rolling down the bridge. The finale, when it finally came, was thunderous, overwhelming, countless bombs bursting in air. The sheer number of colored formations in the sky, to judge by the hundreds of shells going off, was beyond my capacity to imagine. When it was all done, the seniors began to shuffle back inside. At ground level the horns and shouting must have been deafening.

The crowd returning from the waterfront filled the streets, and getting home was an adventure. It was like being caught up in an evacuation, though the atmosphere was anything but somber. The mood was infectious, and we shared in the collective jubilation as we made our way home.

Below our bedroom the throng continued to stream toward the subway. Claire lit a candle, but I imagined we lay under a pyrotechnic sky. Not the one we had just witnessed, but a firmament lighted at intervals by a solitary shell, each one different from the last in color and formation.

By midnight the exodus was complete, Claire was asleep, and the street had returned to the quiet of the previous night. Remembering the dazzling sliver of green, I hoped I would hold on to that image forever.

A foghorn reverberated in the harbor, like those I had heard when falling asleep as a child on Fishers Island. Goose stirred on his bed, and I reached down to scratch behind his ear. Kissing Claire before turning over, I recalled what Freddy had said about love at the end of our last session. Walking with him to the door, we both smiled in anticipation of the words he always repeated before leaving, his favorite line from W. H. Auden's "Atlantis," "Stagger onward, rejoicing."